Change Your $tory

Noelle Schwantes

Thank you for always believing in me. I love you so very much.
Noelle

SQUARE TREE PUBLISHING
www.squaretreepublishing.com

Copyright © 2021 by Noelle Schwantes

All rights reserved, including the right of reproduction in whole or in part in any form.

Unless otherwise noted, Scripture quotations are taken from the Holy Bible, New International Version®, NIV®. Copyright © 1973, 1978, 1984, 2011 by Biblica, Inc.™ Used by permission of Zondervan. All rights reserved worldwide. www.zondervan.com. The "NIV" and "New International Version" are trademarks registered in the United States Patent Office by Biblica, Inc.™

Scripture quotations marked AMP are from the Amplified® Bible (AMP). Copyright © 2015 by The Lockman Foundation. Used by permission. (www.Lockman.org)

Scripture quotations marked AMPC are from the Amplified® Bible (AMPC). Copyright © 1954, 1958, 1962, 1964, 1965, 1987 by The Lockman Foundation. Used by permission. (www.Lockman.org)

Scripture quotations marked NASB are from the New American Standard Bible®. Copyright © 1960, 1962, 1963, 1968, 1971, 1972, 1973, 1975, 1977, 1995 by The Lockman Foundation. Used by permission. (www.Lockman.org)

Scripture quotations marked ESV are from the ESV® Bible (The Holy Bible, English Standard Version®). Copyright © 2001 by Crossway, a publishing ministry of Good News Publishers. Used by permission. All rights reserved.

Scripture quotations marked MSG are from *The Message*. Copyright © by Eugene H. Peterson 1993, 2002, 2018. Used by permission of NavPress, represented by Tyndale House Publishers, Inc. All rights reserved.

First Square Tree Publishing paperback edition 2022

For more information about bulk purchases, please contact Square Tree Publishing at info@squaretreepublishing.com.

Cover design by Sharon Marta

ISBN 978-1-7353859-4-5

Dedication

To My Boys

Marcel, for being the husband who believes in me unceasingly and has sacrificed and backed me at every turn. This book is a reality in large part because of your belief in me.

Joseph, my funny, tender, precious boy. God gave me this material while you were in my belly, and I pray you see us walk these concepts out until they are living and breathing in you as well.

To Emily Thompson

A prayer request for God to show us the car he wanted us to have. A call from you about a car. A tornado and an insurance payment. Seed for sowing comes from just about anywhere!

Acknowledgments

Sherry Ward and the team at Square Tree Publishing. The basic manuscript for this book was written years ago. I knew it needed to be published and prayed for the right team to do it. I asked for people who followed God and who I could trust—not only to understand and be passionate about the message, but to also have their own passion for spreading Kingdom messages. God answered my prayers with you.

Mom and Dad. Over the years, I've seen many parents push their kids into doing something "safe or productive." I've seen clients waste years in a career they hated because they thought it was what they "should" do. There has never been one moment where you pushed me to do anything other than follow God's plan for my life. This book is the result, and I am so grateful God gave me you both.

During my freshman year of high school, my English teacher, Pam Gatling, had us write our first term paper. She graded us separately on each step…notecards with references, outline, etc. I remember thinking that it was a good skillset for when I wrote my first book. Turns out that it was. Thanks, Mrs. Gatling.

Mary Thompson-Johns. During the darkest time of my life, someone suggested I get a mentor who had what I wanted. You lit up the room with your heart and passion. You still do. There aren't words for what we've walked through together, and I am forever proud and honored to call you sister.

Pedro and Suzette Adao and the 100X team and Community. After many years of trying to figure out how to launch and run a business on my own, I asked God to send someone to help. He sent you. Everything good that has happened for my business has come from the root of kingdom and family. I'm forever grateful and just getting started.

The Prayer Mamas. We have challenged each other, seen the best and the worst, gotten frustrated, talked it through, and most of all, we have prayed. I love you.

Clients. I can't use your names, but you know who you are. I went into my field with the conviction that I would never ask my clients to do something that I wasn't willing to walk through myself. Your questions and struggles challenged me to pursue answers for myself and for you. Thank you for trusting me with your journeys.

Kathy and Bill Hammond (Katie and Emily). Any entrepreneur who says they raised themselves up by their bootstraps isn't telling the truth. The journey isn't easy and demands a deep level of commitment. The Hammond family is a large piece of how Marcel and I made it. Emily and Lance designed the website, Katie helped edit the book, and Bill and Kathy slipped us cash during a period where we didn't know how we would pay the bills. Over all the practical help was draped prayer, forgiveness, and belief in what God had called us to do.

Table of Contents

Chapter 1 ~ Beliefs   21

Chapter 2 ~ Listening to God   47

Chapter 3 ~ Fear   69

Chapter 4 ~ Shame   79

Chapter 5 ~ Stepping into Authority with Your Money   103

Chapter 6 ~ Investing/Educating   123

Chapter 7 ~ Gratitude/Praise/Play   141

Conclusion   151

Praise for *Change Your $tory*

"With bold vulnerability, this book highlights the spiritual and emotional sediment that influences poor thinking and decisions about money. With truth, grace and wisdom, Schwantes equips the reader to do one simple thing: heal"

Julia M. Winston, M.Ed.
CEO & Chief Alignment Advisor
BRAVE Leadership Consulting

"Noelle as a trained trauma therapist and deeply spiritual, intuitive teacher shares her own struggle and relationship with money. As a 20+ year wealth practitioner working with many dozens of individuals and families, I've seen firsthand how social, emotional and spiritual considerations can help or hurt your financial journey. Noelle's wisdom is simple yet profound. Whatever your experience, Noelle provides practical insights that illuminate how to change your financial story."

Stefanie Crowe
Founder and CEO
Aegle Wealth

"Read the book; learn the lessons; master the money. Noelle's writing syle is clear and sharp. Her brave honesty pours through these pages, leaving you with truth, power, and the plans to make your way. Change Your $tory is deep and real, while remaining rich and easy to understand. Women and men alike will be rewarded by this book. Read this and win your money war."

Stephen K De Silva, CPA (retired)
Author and Founder of Prosperous Soul Ministries and Financial Sozo

Prologue

One of my earliest memories is sitting and squirming in church while the pastor spoke. He was teaching about Solomon's request for wisdom and God's pleasure in that request. I stopped squirming when I heard about how Solomon dealt with the two women arguing over the baby. Even as a young child, I was impressed with that bit of brilliance. I became fully alert when the pastor went on to explain that, because of the selflessness of Solomon's request in asking to rule well, God rewarded him. Solomon became one of the richest men in Earth's history. With a strange combination of earthly desire and childlike faith, I remember sitting in the pew, thinking if I asked God for wisdom my request would be "holy" and I would get rich at the same time. There was no question in my mind that God wouldn't answer my request, and so I whispered, "God, make me wise."

So began my journey toward wisdom and financial peace and prosperity. As a child, my motives were certainly suspect. I grew and developed in my walk with God. Whenever anyone made the comment, "That was wise," in response to something I had said, I would smile internally and think about the grace of God that answered a child's request, even with mixed motives.

I grew up in what most would consider an upper-middle-class home. My parents were both educated and gainfully employed, and I went to private Christian schools. I had what I needed and most of what I wanted. If you have read the book, *Rich Dad, Poor Dad*, you may have a picture of what our lives were like. When I was young, my parents struggled with debt and living within our means. My father's dad died when he was two years old, and he grew up with a mom who worked hard to provide, with very little extra and no lessons on finances…especially not wealth building. My father's way of showing love was (and still is) gift giving, and he took great pleasure in giving us the things we wanted, often surprising us with the thoughtfulness of things we hadn't asked for.

Although we had what we needed, it often came at the cost of debt, and I regularly heard the phrase, "We don't have money for that." Somewhere along the way, I developed my parents' habits and also developed a great deal of anxiety about finances. I suspect that many of you reading this might relate to my story. It seems that nothing in the world scares us, shames us, or has us running to medicate our pain faster than fears about money.

Fast forward to my late 20's. My marriage had fallen apart, and I was on my own for the first time in my life. After many years of struggling, I left my marriage rather suddenly. I had about two weeks' worth of clothes and that was about it. I slept on a friend's couch and used to wake up in the middle of the night, feeling like there was an angry snake in my belly. I was also struggling with money like never before. Being emotionally wrecked from the fallout of my marriage, I needed to attend support groups and counseling to keep from going completely off the deep end. Because of that, I chose a job as a server in a restaurant. That job offered the flexibility I needed, but I had very little to live on, and I didn't have a car. I couldn't see a way out of the pain I was in and had lost the drive to live. There had always been money worries before, but I had a dual income home and credit cards. Those things were gone now.

During that painful time, a few pivotal events happened. I began to seek God out of desperation rather than seeking Him with a self-righteous motive of checking prayer off my to-do list. I instead sought healing and peace. I was also listening for responses and listening to the wisdom of people whose lives seemed to be working for them. My faith started to look alive, whereas before, I had been a good model of a legalist— all about the rules and no actual relationship or intimacy. I started to hear God speak to me and guide me.

At some point, it became clear to me that on top of the pain of a failed relationship, the things that kept me tied in knots most were issues connected to money. I was sick of wanting things I couldn't afford and obsessing on how to get them anyway. I was sick of credit card bills and fear about not being able to pay rent. I was sick of feeling that my life and dreams were totally defined by my bank account. I was sick of feeling afraid all the time. In a moment of insight, I prayed a prayer that changed the course of my life. I asked God to help me learn 100% financial surrender. That request is important to remember for what happened later! I had come far enough in my healing to realize that, when I surrendered, peace came, and I wanted that desperately for my finances. I needed Him to Change My $tory.

The next pivotal event happened one day while talking to God about my finances. I felt His now familiar still, small voice whisper, I would be wealthy. It wasn't audible, but just a thought I knew didn't come from me! It startled me so much I jerked my head up, looked at the sky, and said, "Well, don't give it to me now. I can't be trusted with it." I was in a cycle of spending to medicate my fear or any other negative feelings I was having. I knew any money that came my way would get swallowed up in my never-ending need to feel better. Even if it was just for a little while a new book, a fabulous pair of shoes, or a dinner out with the current "man of my dreams" spending distracted me from my pain. And I was trapped in that cycle, which in the end, only exacerbated my fears. We are told in Scripture that if we ask for things in Jesus' name, and in His will, the answer is yes[1]. It was very clear that my financial surrender was in His will because, after praying that prayer, things began to move quickly.

---

1. John 14:14 (AMP)

Not long before praying this prayer, I had started living in the guest house of a couple who had been regulars at the restaurant where I worked. I stayed in their beautiful guest house on an amazing estate. In exchange for free rent, I helped clean weekly and watched the estate when he and his wife were out of town. I also had the opportunity to observe their habits and learn the steps my surrogate uncle had taken to become extremely wealthy. "Uncle Doug" was a natural teacher and was always happy to answer questions and share his knowledge.

He also helped me find a used but very dependable old Nissan Sentra. I had been driving a car so old and beat up, I left it open regularly, hoping that someone would steal it. This "new to me" Sentra was a huge blessing. I kept this car even after I moved out.

One evening, a few days after praying this prayer about financial surrender, a few friends and I were getting ready to leave the house to get something to eat. It was a beautiful balmy night and, as we argued over whether to get Italian or Mexican food, we heard an immense crack. A moment later, my little basement apartment shook. My friend, Craig, went outside to investigate and came in a minute later. He stated that a tree had fallen on top of my "new" car. I laughed, knowing Craig's tendency to pull a prank, but when he insisted, my stomach dropped. I ran outside. Sure enough, a tree, nearly 90 feet tall, had randomly fallen across two large neighboring yards and into my driveway, damaging nothing except my car. There was no wind, no storm, and nothing else damaged. It just "happened" to fall at that moment.

    Thinking of my recent request of financial surrender, I looked up at the sky and said, "What in the %$#!?" As a general rule, I don't recommend using profanity with God. What I do recommend, though, is that you are real with Him. And, in that moment, I was very real. It's difficult to be anything less than authentic when you're in the middle of a moment of total panic! See, the car wasn't just a car to me. It was safety. It was control. My life had completely fallen apart, and all I had was that car. I had gone several months without any transportation when I first left my marriage, and the car meant I had a way of escape if I was scared. It was the freedom of never being trapped. God knew all this. He also knew that the fastest way to answer my prayer was to take the car away and begin to answer my prayer for total financial surrender. Those lessons eventually led to finding peace in any circumstance around my finances, an important asset to have if you dream of working for yourself and changing the world with your business! There are lots of ups and downs on that journey!

    A few days later, I realized all of this and brokenly whispered, "I want to learn to surrender more than I wanted that car." And I meant it. These days I picture a rather large and emphatic cheer from all of heaven when I uttered that statement. I didn't realize it then, but that statement opened up the door for me to be ready to fulfill my calling. It was a turning point, and I wouldn't be where I am today if I had chosen differently.

The book that follows simply chronicles the things God has taught my heart. Over the years, I had well-meaning friends get uncomfortable when I stated that God told me I'd be wealthy. Maybe you feel some of the same things as you read this! This book isn't about that, but it will open up the spiritual lessons that need to happen for you to step into that without any anxiety or striving. It WILL teach the lessons and clear the baggage that may have kept you from stepping fully into your purpose. These unconscious obstacles have kept you from pursuing your dreams successfully. The chapters in this book will tell *my* story, and at times, the stories of others who have learned similar lessons. What's the main lesson, specifically? You were created for peace and power around your finances, no matter what they look like right now. No matter how bad you are at budgeting, because girls, I've never found a budget I couldn't destroy! You need to clear the emotional and spiritual baggage that keeps you from financial power, abundance, and your calling and dreams. This book will provide a scriptural basis for these lessons. And for those of you who really want to let the information sink into your brain chemistry, there will be information on resources to guide you on your journey.

I heard a pastor share that, in the Hebrew culture, they knew what their calling was based on the wounds of their past. Ladies, (and Gentlemen) God won't waste your past. You aren't selfish for having a dream of something beyond what you're experiencing today. God planted that dream in you.

Now in the 6th grade, I had a mad crush on Stephen Thurmond. The first time I laid eyes on him, it was as if time stopped for a moment and light from heaven bathed his face. You think I'm kidding, but I'm entirely serious. I went on to make a total fool of myself over this boy (and a few others over the years, if I'm honest). The crush lasted through high school, although I learned to hide it…I had my pride after all. How many times do you think I begged God for Stephen to feel the same way about me? This dream wasn't answered, and in hindsight, I know that was an incredibly good thing for reasons that I won't go into now. Stephen and I are happily married to other people these days. This story's point is that, until I did a lot of heart healing around my relationship with men, I didn't see the brokenness in me. That brokenness was running my craving regarding men.

At its core, this book is about heart healing where finances are concerned. We have our Dave Ramseys teaching us good financial habits, but who talks about the brokenness we bring to the lessons? I could never seem to institute his suggestions because of my own beliefs and wounds. How was I to launch a vision when I felt having money was tainted or evil? How did I pursue income when I believed, on some level, it was wrong to have? The answer was that I spent it as fast as I got it. How did I believe I had anything to offer the world when my core identity said I had to run harder and perform better than anyone else (even though I could never quite pull it off)? That particular belief landed me in the hospital as a senior in high school, burnt out, and in treatment at 18 years old.

Your dream and calling are waiting on the other side of heart healing in an area you've probably never looked at this way before…money.

I'm not a natural money manager. The fact that I've written a book on this topic is almost laughable. You want to know why I've done it? Why I burn for this topic and ache for your heart to understand the concepts? I ache for you to take hold of the flickering flame inside of you the dream, the itch, the vision to have an impact. Build the business, the non-profit, the program, the event. God put something in you. He planned it for you before the foundations of the earth. It is vital that your heart heals so you can share that healing with a broken world. Anything outside of that means we are sharing out of our brokenness, and nobody needs any more of that!

I write the edits for this book in the middle of a broken time. The coronavirus has kept the world isolated and in fear for a few months now. Domestic abuse has risen, businesses are failing. George Floyd was killed by a police officer, and riots are breaking out across the United States. The world desperately needs answers for what is available in your healed heart.

You are absolutely free to ride it out. You can post on social media, have some wine, or drown the anxiety while binge-watching Hulu. Or you can face your pain, allow the Holy Spirit to walk you through healing, and step up to the flame in your heart that just won't die. That flame is the Creator of the Universe calling you forward, asking you to see yourself through His eyes and have the audacity to believe His amazing plans for you.

A Note About Financial Abundance

As I wrote this book, I was initially concerned about being attacked for preaching a prosperity gospel. It seems the evangelical world's favorite targets of late are those who dare to teach about prosperity. They infer that if we follow God, He will make all of us rich, as if being rich is the best life has to offer. How is it possible to teach about stewarding wealth while walking the fine line of not focusing on wealth as the goal? I believe the answer to this fine line is in the definition of financial abundance. Financial abundance is not about how much you have; it is about the peace you have. It is about having enough to fully fulfill the calling God has on your life.

It could be stated that the bigger the calling is, the more money it will need to fuel it. I have friends whose callings do not include a lot of financial prosperity in terms of wealth. They don't really want it. They live simply. And frankly, they don't want the added responsibility that stewarding a lot of money involves. On the other hand, I also have friends who have been called to steward large amounts of money. They have learned to submit it all to God and use the resources they have to make the world a better place. They have learned that money is simply a tool, and it doesn't hold any power over them. This book *is* about a prosperity gospel. But this book differs in the knowledge that there is *nothing* in this world to satisfy the heart like relationship and intimacy with God. When we have that, we are prosperous in the richest sense of the word, and everything else is given to us out of that richness.

    I believe there are those who God blesses with wealth. Scripture is full of people and lessons about stewarding wealth for God's glory. Pedro Adao, one of my mentors, said the following while we were on a Zoom call. He was sharing about how so many people say, "I just want enough for my family and myself." I was internally nodding my head. I have heard countless people say things to that effect and didn't necessarily disagree with the sentiment. The next moment literally snapped my head back as Pedro said, in that passionate way of his, "That is the most selfish thing I've ever heard!"

Wait, *what*?
    He went on to describe that there are millions in need in our world. Not having a heart to impact them (or wanting to have the income to help them) is, in fact, selfish!

So, let's think a minute about this...that dream you have for a business or a ministry. What if someone is waiting for you to step into your calling so they can get the help they need? If God placed it in you, there is someone in the world who needs it and is waiting for it. This book talks about the heart healing that needs to happen for you to boldly move forward into what you were designed to do. It is what you need to be safe and at peace in wealth. Yes, it feels risky and takes a spiritual development some people aren't willing to face. But, for those of us who understand the true definition of prosperity, it is a place of humble willingness and joy to impact the kingdom for God's glory. May you find the path in these pages.

Chapter 1

Beliefs

---◆●◆---

There is something in you that is meant to change the world. Start by changing your story.

I grew up believing there was never enough money for what I wanted. There was a hole in my soul. I never felt I was good enough, no matter how hard I worked, but the debt that fueled my compulsive spending tried to fill in the gap. It was all unspoken; I wasn't even conscious of this belief until I was an adult buried in debt…for the third time. I also grew up believing that money—or even a desire for it—was wrong. My beliefs and faulty identity, more than any other factor, impacted my choices regarding money. And because they were faulty, the results were very painful. Those beliefs, and the core identity that told me I had to continually prove myself good enough, demanded I spent money as fast as I got it. I felt it was wrong to want or have it, so I certainly couldn't keep it! The real kicker was that the belief fueling this cycle was unconscious. I wasn't even aware of how those thoughts fueled my actions. As my career and income advanced, so did my spending. And because of that, my dream and calling were always postponed.

In this chapter, we're going to tackle those beliefs holding you back from the plans God has for you, and we're going to get them straightened out. It's time, ladies. Before we dive into that though, take a moment to go to (www.changeyourfinancialstory.com/resources) and take the beliefs assessment listed. This will give you a good baseline to figure out why you haven't been getting the results you want in your financial life.

The Kingdom

A foundational component that needs to be in place is for you to have an accurate understanding of the term "kingdom" as it's used in Scripture. For years, I struggled to understand why I didn't see anyone who had the authority and power the disciples displayed in the New Testament. I'd read the story in Luke 10, where Jesus told the disciples He had given them all authority and that they would do even greater things than He had done. Several years ago, I read this again for what felt like the first time. I began to seriously ask why I, (and dare I say the Christian church at large), weren't experiencing this authority. I started to dig deeper. Through a conversation with a friend who was researching what the kingdom of God looked like, I stumbled onto a realization. While I thought the kingdom of God was heaven, it was something completely different than I had ever considered.

I grew up reading Scripture and thinking the kingdom of God was always referring to heaven, but after digging into this idea of authority and what comes with the Kingdom of God, I realized that the Kingdom isn't necessarily a place.

In the original language, 'Kingdom' in most New Testament Scriptures is *basileia* which means, "the right to rule, royal power, dominion." Also known as authority! The entire framework of this book rests on a Kingdom concept. You were designed to live in authority and this includes your finances. Dubb Alexander describes the Kingdom this way, "The Kingdom is the heart and authority of God on earth through me."

In Matthew 25:34 Jesus said, "Come, you who are blessed by my Father; take your inheritance, the kingdom (*basilieia*) prepared for you since the creation of the world." The authority we are talking about today was prepared for you before the foundation of the world was formed. It was the plan from the very beginning. Charles Kraft, in his book, *I Give You Authority*, says most Christians aren't experiencing *basilieia* because they don't even know they have it. Some of you may be thinking what I used to think, "the inheritance is what I'll get in heaven." You may have an expectation that things are going to be miserable or only somewhat tolerable while we're here on earth. Matthew 6:10 tells us we are to pray, "Your Kingdom come, Your will be done, on earth as it is in heaven." Jesus instructed his disciples to pray this way. He followed up in Luke 10, telling them that He had given them all authority to trample on snakes and scorpions and the ability to exercise authority over the power of the enemy.

Notice we still have to deal with them. He's not offering a life without battle. The first time Jesus sent them out after telling them this, they came back joyful because, "Even the demons are subject to us in Your name!" They experienced the joyful rush of authority in Christ. Later on, just before He went back to heaven, Jesus told the disciples He was sending the Holy Spirit and they would do even greater things than He had. The bar is set high in the very best way. These Scriptures paint a picture of victory and strength here on earth. God's plan for us is to live in peace and victory, abundant life, here on earth. We are to push back the darkness and help share this path to peace and victory for others who are struggling. Money has a role to play in that. But we can't participate in God's plan for us to steward our money and be part of the fight against darkness if we are living as victims who don't know the laws God has put in place for the Kingdom and how that impacts our finances. We have to know how to partner with God and to use the authority He's given us. Now that we've laid a foundation around the kingdom, let's look at some texts that have given us the idea that money is evil or wrong.

Does God Say Money Is Evil?

We'll start with Hebrews 13:5 (AMPC). It says the following: "Let your character or moral disposition be free from love of money [including greed, avarice, lust, and craving for earthly possessions] and be satisfied with your present [circumstances and with what you have]; for He [God] Himself has said, I will not in any way fail you nor give you up nor leave you without support. [I will] not, [I will] not, [I will] not in any degree leave you helpless nor forsake nor let [you] down (relax my hold on you)! [Assuredly not!]"

This verse is a simple direction not to put our love toward something that will let us down and keep us unfulfilled. It doesn't say to be free from money; we are to be free from the *love* of it. Money is amoral, like a table or a chair. The risk comes when we give it power over us it's not meant to have. That leads to pain. God says very emphatically in this passage that He won't let us down, financially or in any other way. So, a love of money is unnecessary. The vital issue here is, do we believe He means this? If we find ourselves worried or freaked out when a financial obstacle arises, we don't fully believe this text in our hearts. This is also why God promised to write his promises on our hearts.[1] When you find a promise that you can't fully believe, God promised to take care of that as well.

Another text often used to discourage wealth is Matthew 19:24-26 (AMPC) (You can also find this story in the Gospel of Mark and Luke.)

"Again I tell you, it is easier for a camel to go through the eye of a needle than for a rich man to go into the Kingdom of heaven. When the disciples heard this, they were utterly puzzled (astonished, bewildered), saying 'Who then can

---

1. Jeremiah 31:33

be saved [from eternal death]?' But Jesus looked at them and said, 'With men this is impossible, but all things are possible with God.'" It is true that finances have a risk of becoming an idol. But I would suggest that your focus of this text should be on all things being possible with God.

So, is this book fundamentally wrong? Am I luring people away from their salvation to even suggest a focus on finances? Here's the deal: it is quite possible for you to launch a business and build wealth by learning good principles and working hard. That direction though, tends to include a whole lot of stress and struggle. If you're uncertain about the truth of that statement, ask any entrepreneur with a "pull yourself up by the bootstraps" mentality. It's a hard road. And the biggest struggle is often the uncertainty and dark voice going on between the ears. What I advocate is doing the heart work around money and getting your beliefs straight so that you know when you're being lied to. Doing heart work takes surrendering this area to have the peace and confidence that is intended for you. It takes knowing in your spirit, soul, and intellect that the wealth you have is God's and you are just the steward who sends it out as He directs. Money is not the problem. Our beliefs, attitudes, and focus towards it are. I believe it is the heart work around money that makes stewarding wealth in partnership with God an "all things are possible" equation.

For those of you who think Scripture is very clearly against wealth, try these on for size. In Genesis 13, we hear how Abram became very wealthy as he followed God. In Genesis 26, Isaac reaped a hundredfold from his crops because God blessed him. Jacob gained wealth in Genesis, despite the fact that his father-in-law was continually trying to cheat him. In Deuteronomy, God brought an entire nation into wealth in the promised land (when they finally learned their lessons and trusted Him). God made Solomon rich because He was pleased with Solomon's request for wisdom. In 1 Chronicles, God established a kingdom under Jehoshaphat's control and gave him great wealth and honor. There are many more examples, and I encourage you to dig deeply into the stories as you begin to question and change your beliefs about money. Next, I want to talk a little more about the attitudes we tend to have regarding finances.

Poverty Spirit Vs. Mammon

I usually describe our journeys with money to clients around the imagery that God has an ideal plan for us regarding finances. Picture it as God's ideal road or path for you. It involves peace, joy, plenty for giving…basically everything we need to fulfill the call and plans He has for our lives. So, that vision you have for a business? Yes, it's already pre-funded.

With that ideal road in mind, there are also ditches on each side of the road. The enemy makes it his business to get us to travel in one or both of those ditches. Some of us have spent most of our driving time in those ditches! The ditch that most Christians tend to fall into is what I call a "poverty spirit." Many Christians use this term (although you won't find the two words specifically linked in Scripture). The term denotes an inclination of mind and character, and the basic message is, "There is never enough." Think of all the areas in our culture where this is the belief. How many are connected to religious life? How many people have been chased out of churches because they were disgusted by the guilt-filled, manipulative call for offering? Many Christians and churches have bought into Satan's lie that there isn't enough; that God isn't enough because He doesn't keep His promises. In the earth's system, that may be true, but in the Kingdom, there is abundance. When we learn to live in that system, we are released from the poverty spirit. So, what does a poverty spirit look like on a practical level? How do you know if it's impacting your finances and dreams?[2]

The poverty spirit:
- Self-defeats
- Shames
- Steals power from us
- Wraps you in fear
- Keeps us a "nobody"
- Creates anxiety
- Hoards things
- Makes you feel trapped
- Chokes generosity

[2]. Poverty Spirit, Spirit of Mammon, Lies, and Dominions lists all adapted from Stephen DeSilva's Material in *Money and the Prosperous Soul*

Beliefs

- Hides you
- Enslaves you
- Robs you of your dreams

The poverty spirit doesn't have good fruit. That in itself tells us this perspective isn't from God. This perspective also flies in the face of God's promises to "supply all our needs according to His riches in glory." He asks us to seek His kingdom and righteousness first and promises to give us the food, drink, and clothes that we need.[3][4] When you look at the attributes of the poverty spirit above, how many items on the list are true in your own life right now? How many of them are true in your family and religious history?

Around the time I began researching the concepts for this book, my husband Marcel and I asked God to put us fully into our callings. I will never forget sitting at our kitchen table with my pregnant belly pressing against the edge. We told God we were sick of the status quo and asked Him to move us forward into what He created us to do. What followed was what I look back on as our "specialty training." You could say this was phase 2 of my request for 100% total surrender. The day after we prayed that prayer, my husband was notified that he would be laid off from his lucrative corporate job. As I began to write this book, we had to move out of our home and rent it to people who could afford it, moving in with my parents. Prior to that, Marcel and I went

---

3. Philippians 4:19

4. Matthew 6: 31-33

through our savings and cashed out the last of our retirement accounts. We were sued for medical bills because we were late one too many times. We had to sell our car and learned how to juggle staying in integrity and calling about bills we weren't able to pay on time. At one point we wondered if we were going to have to file for bankruptcy.

Into the second year of this journey, we were working on our taxes. For various reasons it was put off, so we were up late at night finishing off all the details. With a sigh of relief, the submit button was finally pushed and, after a moment of buffering, the website popped up at a new location. Our mouths dropped open when we realized TurboTax had rerouted us to the food stamps page. There was a beat of silence in which both of us were trying to decide whether to laugh or cry. Without a word, we both chose the laughter option and one of us hysterically pointed out that you know you're really broke when the tax software suggests you file for food stamps.

There were moments without laughter. Moments when I was furious with God about the pain we were in. In hindsight, I now know there were things that needed to be exposed in me. Those things could have gotten in the way of me fully believing and living what I now teach. I think of it as God making my head knowledge into heart knowledge. This is what God meant when He said He would write His promises on our hearts.[5] It isn't meant to be intellectual

---

5. Jeremiah 31:33

knowledge alone, it is meant to be something we know on an experiential, cellular level.

Core Beliefs

Now maybe you're thinking, "I recognize this poverty spirit as something impacting me, but I can fix it by changing my attitude or by speaking affirmations, etc." Here is the problem with that: If your attitude isn't built on something you truly believe, studies by the University of Waterloo in Canada have shown that this actually increases stress on the body. Your body knows when you're lying to yourself and doing that will set you up for disease![6] Here's an example: many people have had a therapist or friend tell them to practice repeating affirmations if there is an area they struggle with. So, if you struggle with the poverty spirit and don't fully believe (yet) that God will supply all your needs, affirmations physically hurt you! Repeating "God will supply all my needs" without addressing your doubts, injures your body. Even in this small example, your beliefs make it work or fail!

So, what do we do? It's important to have positive beliefs, but if we lie and tell ourselves something we don't believe in our core, it causes additional stress and disease in our bodies. Here is the answer: the only way to truly change ourselves is to change our core belief. Another way to look at this concept is to think of our financial lives as a fruit tree.

---

6. *The Healing Code*, Alexander Lyon

Change Your $tory

Ask yourself, are you getting the financial results/fruit that you want in your life? If not, you can't fix that by constantly chopping the fruit off the tree. You have to fix the root system. This is why so many have been frustrated by an inability to follow through on feedback from books, financial planners, etc. The advice you got, while it may have been wise and good, couldn't be implemented in a toxic root system. Earnie Larsen, a well-known writer and speaker on recovery from addictions, said in a workshop, "You can't outrun your core belief." You can't outrun your roots. You must heal them. This idea is why nothing has worked in the past. Why you keep feeling kicked back into old problems or behaviors, why you failed to launch the dream, the reason you can't seem to stick to a budget. Nobody has been teaching you to deal with the heart, the root issues around money. The journey is rigorous, and you may feel scared or uncertain. But the great news is, when you dig into this process, when you commit and take action toward healing your root beliefs about money, your dreams are waiting on the other side.

If you believe there is never enough, it will define your reality. You'll never overcome your fear of lack until you change what you listen to. "Take care what you listen to. By your standard of measure it will be measured to you; and more will be given to you besides."[7] The ramifications of this are astounding. The things you tell yourself, the people you listen to (whatever they are saying), is what you will get—and not just in the measure you listen, but exponentially. It's as simple as this, tell yourself you're broke, listen to the news

---

7. Mark 4:24 (NASB)

about all the financial catastrophes in our world (there are plenty to choose from), and you will receive what you listen to.

Maybe you want to argue with me here, "I *am* broke. There *are* financial catastrophes." Part of the issue around that argument is that those struggles happen when we agree to live under the earth's cursed system, rather than agreeing and living in the Kingdom's system. This walk I'm talking about is full of paradoxes, too. One of them is that we are to walk by faith and not by sight. What does Scripture tell you about your needs? About provision? This book is basically about learning to trust God's word regarding your finances, allowing Him to write it on your heart in such a way that it is experiential knowledge instead of intellectual knowledge. When it becomes experiential knowledge, it's unshakeable because we have lived it. From that place, your story will change. Take a moment to think about what voices you listen to about finances. Do you want more of what those voices are saying? If not, you can start to change your beliefs by researching and listening to different voices. Listen to the people who have what you want. Many years ago, when my life was coming apart at the seams, I became desperate for healing. I was so determined to be healed I decided it would be my primary goal. Anything else was going to be secondary. It had to be, because I was a total basket case. I started going to 12-step meetings to deal with some of the compulsive issues in my life. In those meetings, I was encouraged to pick a sponsor to walk with me through my healing, and it was suggested that I pick someone who had what I wanted. It was pretty simple, and some of the best advice I've ever gotten. I now call the woman who sponsored me "sister." And today, I have the gifts that I saw and needed in her. The point—start to change your beliefs by listening to voices who have what you want.

Another way to start clear out your root system is to get into Scripture for yourself. By listening to these new voices, you can start to question some of the poverty spirit ideas you've received from religion, your family system, your culture, etc.

When Our Experience Seems to Prove God/Scripture Can't Be Trusted

All of us grew up in families that dealt with money. All of us grew up with certain cultural, family, and religious belief systems around this topic. For our purposes, we'll call the beliefs "agreements." Agreements are things we have experienced and believe to be true, so we have "made an agreement" with that belief in our hearts. Many Christians grow up with the agreement that it is unholy to be wealthy. Suppose we reach beyond the topic of money. In that case, an agreement that can interfere with our ability to be in deeper relationship with God can be the agreement that God is not trustworthy.

Agreements are sometimes hard to identify because they are rooted in experiences from the past. They feel absolutely true because of experiences Satan throws at us to make us doubt. Often, they are underlying beliefs we don't even realize we believe. For example, someone who was abused as a child may have made the agreement that God is not trustworthy because where was God when he/she was being abused? Agreements can be so deep-rooted and strong, you may find you need support from a professional to work through them. If you recognize some of these issues at work in your life and want to start dealing with them immediately, I recommend you go to changeyourfinancial-story.com/resources and download a free resource list with some authors and options for diving into your healing. You can also sign up to be notified when we do our next online event. One thing I can guarantee, God's word *can* be trusted, and if you search and address agreements that are not in line with Scripture, you will be on the path to peace that passes understanding and a life of purpose and joy. It will start to happen automatically.

Now, what about the other side of the ditch?

Spirit of Mammon

"No one can serve two masters; for either he will hate the one and love the other, or he will hold to one and despise the other. You cannot serve God and mammon."[8] Many people have grown up feeling that money is evil because of a misunderstanding of this passage. Take note; the New Testament contains 215 passages pertaining to faith, about 218 about salvation, and, depending on whom you ask, more

---

8. Matthew 6:24 (NASB)

than 2084 on stewardship and accountability for finances. How we relate to money is one of the strongest litmus tests for our hearts. Money makes us more of whatever we are.

Another aspect of this concept was discovered by Ron Smith, who found that in the Canaanite culture at the time of Jesus, Philistines worshipped a god of finance called, in Aramaic, mammon. Based on this, we posit that mammon may actually be a demonic spirit in Satan's kingdom. God has power; the spirit of mammon has power. Money has no power; it is simply a tool. Your trajectory will be defined by the power you choose to follow. Craig Hill states in his book, *Living on the Third River*, "Until you realize the impotence of money, you will never be free from its pursuit, nor from the influence and dominion of the spirit behind it." What does it look like when our belief system is aligned with mammon?

Mammon:
- Self Aggrandizes
- Flatters
- Fans the flames of lust and greed
- Uses wealth to attract people to us and instills a basic insecurity of being loved only because of what we can offer
- Believes it can buy connections and has an inflated sense of power
- Inflames a desire to posses
- Destroys loyalty
- Demands allegiance to money and self
- Encourages sensual living

- Creates an entitlement to comfort
- Focuses on image

If you put your peace in riches or anything else other than God, you are setting yourself up for pain and disappointment. Why? Because no one but God is fully capable of guiding you without letting you down. We see this happen all the time. People fall in love and believe that person will never hurt them, so they give their heart away, only to be devastated with the loss of the relationship. They realize they lost themselves and put their faith in something that harmed them.

How do we get stuck in either of these ditches? The only way Satan can knock us off God's path and plan is if we believe his lies. He is the father of lies. They originated with him. It is simply a list of lies we believe that cause us to falter and be harmed by either of these perspectives. Think about this. Satan has been around since the beginning of earth's history. So, he has watched your family's history since the beginning of time. Given that, do you think he might have a bit of insight into what God's plans are for you? Someone who knows more about your history than you do? Do you think he has had time to come up with some pretty significant lies to thwart all God has for you? This can also be a clue into where God means for us to impact the world…in the area where Satan has most attacked you. That being said, what are some of the lies he uses?

Lies Satan uses:
- I'm afraid of failure, so I can't risk taking this chance
- I have to be perfect. If not, I don't deserve this
- I'm afraid of success; people will expect too much
- I am incapable of stewarding money well
- I have to keep up appearances: I can't be vulnerable
- I don't deserve love, money, health, etc.
- I will always be the poor one in the family
- I'm just a _____ (wife, teacher, mom, etc.)
- I don't deserve to be wealthy
- I deserve to be wealthy (entitlement)
- What I want is too much to ask for
- I am stupid
- I am not talented enough
- God is too big and busy to pay attention to my dream
- Negative thoughts are a part of who I am. I can't control them
- God won't care for me because of my mistakes
- I haven't done enough to earn blessings
- I have to earn my right to be cared for
- I will never be free of sin
- I'm destined to be poor
- I'm overlooked and not charismatic enough
- I will never get out from under the weight of my debt
- It's impossible to live without using debt
- The rich are unhappy
- Wealthy people are selfish
- Wealth equals evil
- Money controls you

- You can't follow God and have money, too.
- I'm not capable of fulfilling my dreams

This list is by no means definitive. What other lies come to mind that you've been believing? If these are some of the lies, what does the ideal look like? Take a moment to think about that. We have grown up seeing poverty or mammon spirit in the world around us, and it seems like there are very few places where we see the principles in the Bible at work. Does this mean the Bible is wrong? Part of what will make this book's messages bear fruit in your life is your belief. What we believe will make or break our results, and that is why this book starts with this chapter.

Let's start by looking at what God's ideal is. Craig Hill uses the term "sparrow faith" to describe the faith we are meant to enjoy.[9] Sparrow faith knows the Bible promises provision, not because we work, but because we are more important to Him than sparrows!

DeSilva shares with us that "when we're spiritually immature, we primarily receive.[10] DeSilva goes on to say...

> But when we reach maturity and dominion, we act as generous benefactors [stewards] distributing the supernatural abundance of our Father's kingdom. This pivotal change or revelation that takes place in us is

---
9. *Living on the Third River*, Craig Hill
10. *Money and the Prosperous Soul*, Stephen DeSilva

that of taking ownership. Jesus told us, "Our Father has chosen gladly to give [us] the kingdom" (Luke 12:32). This promise can seem vague and overwhelming until we see we can't fully manage the family business without having access to its resources. It would be inconceivable for God to authorize Jesus to fulfill his destiny as the Messiah without giving Him the wealth of the Kingdom to back that authority. Likewise, Joseph could hardly oversee his storehouse strategy in Egypt without being able to act as owner of the nations' resources. All authority must be provided with a measure of ownership. And dominion, by definition, requires ownership of a kingdom.

The next obvious question is, how do we take ownership of the Kingdom? What does this look like on a practical level? I mentioned earlier that, for most of my life, I thought the Kingdom in Scripture was referring to heaven. It was a nice thought, but usually, it felt far removed from my life on earth and the solutions I was looking for. It is hard to overstate how excited I felt upon realizing what Kingdom really referred to was an authority I was meant to experience NOW! I was given royal power…now! In terms of how to use this power practically, it's quite simple. "And the Lord said, 'Who then is that faithful and wise manager, whom the master puts in charge of his servants to give them their food allowance at the proper time? It will be good for that servant whom the master finds doing so when he returns. Truly I tell you, he will put him in charge of all his possessions'" (Luke

12:42-44). The way to steward more, to place yourself in a position to be trusted with wealth, is to practice trusting God's promises around provision, now. Listen for His direction in your financial decisions with what you possess today. Practice integrity and obedience to what He places on your heart at this moment. Be a good steward right now with what you currently have. When you're operating in this place, your financial life will have the following characteristics[11]:

- Authority
- Power
- Peace
- Joy
- God as provider/sparrow faith
- You conserve and use with confidence
- You know and plan to be a blessing
- You set goals in conjunction with the Holy Spirit and feel joyful as He reveals the plans
- You have self-control and discipline in reaching goals
- Contentment
- Rest
- Gratitude
- Security
- Your goals come from a heart knowledge of God's presence as your source of joy
- You have unlimited access to wisdom and strength, and you move in the confidence of knowing that
- You revel in generosity without being moved by guilt or

---

11. *Money and the Prosperous Soul*, Stephen DeSilva

manipulation
- You seek continual expansion and growth as the Holy Spirit guides
- You rejoice when others are blessed, knowing there is plenty for everyone

It is at this point some of those agreements we talked about may be rearing their ugly heads. Take a minute to note the characteristics that you find yourself disagreeing with. There may be an internal eye roll, sadness that you won't ever experience God's ideal, or irritation because you don't feel some aspect of this is Biblical. I would invite you to find any statements you disagreed with or reacted emotionally to. I have researched and walked through all of these concepts with God. If I wrote it, I stand behind it. But you have to have it clear in your heart. So start there. If the statement is Scriptural, but you don't trust it or believe it, write down the reasons. Why do you feel the Bible is wrong? What experiences have you had that make these statements seem untrue? Just like that, you have identified some of your agreements. It is important to allow the Holy Spirit to counsel you and change your heart around any beliefs that don't line up with Scripture. As we've said before, you can't outrun your core beliefs, and any beliefs that don't line up with God's reality will trip you up as long as they are allowed to stay. And they aren't just tripping you up; they're actively keeping you from your destiny. It is not the abusive relationship you were in, the alcohol, your perceived lack of skill, etc., that has kept you from your calling. It is your beliefs that don't line up

Beliefs

with who and what God says about you. The alcohol or man, etc. is just what we choose to use to muffle the pain of a life outside of God's kingdom.

If you are striving to change your financial story and, deep down, you don't believe it is possible, you will never be successful. It is absolutely vital that you address this core issue, or you will, in effect, be shooting yourself in the foot over and over again. The good news is, nothing is wrong with you! Your dreams are within reach. It's only your beliefs that need to be adjusted!

The point is, money can easily seduce us away from the core truth that we are fully dependent on God for our peace. If we focus on money instead of God, it is possible we will not make it into heaven or have the peace the Kingdom offers while we're here on earth. Depending on your financial situation right now, you may be thinking something along the lines of, "Easy for you to say, don't focus on money. I have to focus on money. I have bills I need to pay, a vision I want to birth. How am I supposed to avoid focusing on money?!"

This goes back to the idea of agreements and beliefs. The reality is that in the Kingdom, there is more than enough. There is excess. Under the earth's curse system, there is never enough. Think back for a moment to the first time in your life when you believed there might not be enough. As children, we don't develop logic until approximately age seven, and it has been said by many child development experts that children are "keen observers and poor interpreters." A child can catch every detail of an event. But without proper support or instruction, they can easily draw the wrong conclusions. We often find we have developed agreements from a very young age based on lies Satan planted as truths through our experiences. For example, one young man remembers very clearly his father being laid off from a family-owned business. The owner of the business drove a very expensive car and had a beautiful mansion, but told his father they could not afford his salary. The young man remembers the depression that followed as his father struggled to get work. This young man made an agreement based on that experience. He believed, from a very young age, that wealthy people were liars and cheats. Beyond that, he also began to believe God did not supply all his needs. This set up a painful cycle of guilt around a desire to have money (because he didn't want to be a liar and a cheat) and immense pressure to make money because God would not supply what he needed.

What is the outcome of unbelief? The Bible focuses on our belief in God and His promises, but the principle holds the same pragmatically. If I don't believe that God is looking for people to steward His resources, I will either never find it, or, if I do become wealthy, I will be caught in fear and anxiety about how to manage it, someone taking it away, etc. I have a wealthy friend who is a proud atheist. He once told me, "I'm rich, and I have the ulcers to prove it." I've never forgotten his statement. There is another way. There is a path to freedom that doesn't give you ulcers and doesn't include striving, fear, or shame. It is a way of rest and joy.

So what's next? Once you become clearer on an accurate view of finances and have taken some steps toward clearing them up, what's the next step to changing your financial story?

Chapter 2
Listening to God

Listen Like Your Life Depends on It.

In the last chapter, I talked about praying for God to put Marcel and me in our callings and what happened immediately after. What that looked like was Marcel losing his lucrative job and me cutting back on hours (and losing a major portion of my income) because we didn't want to put our son in daycare. During that time, God continued to refine us. As we were pressed, what we really believed in our hearts became very apparent. One particular story sticks in my mind as a great example.

  I had begun working on this book and I had actually woken up one day with the entire outline in my head. That fact alone should give you great comfort. The thought of me writing about finances is almost comical when you look at my financial history. Only God could have given me an entire book in one thought. I had to really hold onto that fact, because, given the financial struggles we were having, I wrestled with the concepts. Over a series of weeks, when one of Marcel's clients was late on a payment, we were sued for medical bills. We were calling creditors almost constantly to arrange payments, and we were two months behind on our car payment. The bank notified us they were days away from repossessing it. I will never forget taking my son Joseph for a walk around the neighborhood that day. I wept as I watched Marcel and my father drive past. They were on the way to the bank so my father could pay the car payments. The next day, we got a credit card bill with $700+ in late fees and interest payments. I had been calling for weeks over a mistake on the statement, and each time I called, I was assured it would be taken care of. Unfortunately, another bill would come with more late fees assessed. To cap it all off, we got a notice that our home was no longer insured due to non-payment of the premiums. I went for another walk with Joseph in the stroller and called my friend Mary, spitting and sobbing into the phone. I venomously stated, "God doesn't supply our needs according to His riches in glory." The ironic thing was, I had already written the rough draft of this book! I was especially mad because I was "taking a stand" for God's promises and felt He had let us down on almost every front. My friend listened and honored my pain. I soon calmed down enough to explain what was going on to my son, who had been looking at me worriedly. Over the next few days, it began to sink in. The best way God provides for me is by increasing my trust in Him. I had to realize that God knows "His riches in glory" are more about my relationship with Him and trust in Him than they are about money.[1] I eventually was able

---

1. Philippians 4:19

to surrender to His plan for provision rather than my own. Even in the face of our need, I was able to trust His promises. I began to see this as the true "riches" God was most concerned about. But that wasn't the end of the story.

One step at a time, the issues got taken care of. The credit card company did take off the fees after a few more phone calls. We cleared up the misunderstanding with the home insurance. Marcel's client finally paid him and we went to court and were granted a continuance of the medical lawsuit. But here's the ringer. A few months earlier, I had felt impressed to file our taxes as soon as possible. I started to do the work, but when it looked like we were going to owe taxes, I got frustrated and abandoned the project. Flash forward to where we had only a day and a half to complete them. We finally sat down, and at about midnight on the due date, we had taken every deduction we could find and got what we owed down to a small fee. We had already set aside more than that for tax payments. Marcel and I were exhausted but relieved to know we would be able to pay that debt come April 15. We hit the button to begin the process to file the taxes, and Turbo Tax (bless that fabulous company) did one last check of the return to look for discrepancies. They found one. We read it over, dreading that this may put our balance owed at more than we were able to pay. It turned out we had misstated that our son had only lived with us for seven months out of the year. As we put a 12 in the box instead of a seven, we watched the marker on the side of the screen move from owing money to receiving a substantial refund. I jerked my head up to look at my dignified husband, standing with his mouth hanging open and a vacant look in his eyes. He was convinced I had done something wrong to screw up all his hard work. After I convinced him this was accurate, I recalled something that stopped me in my tracks. If I had obeyed the impression to do our taxes earlier, we would have had this check come in much sooner. My parents would not have had to pay our car payment, and we would not have had to go to court because we would have been able to pay off the medical debt. Despite what I felt and saw in my reality, God had been taking steps to provide for us. Because I didn't listen and fully obey, that provision had been postponed, and we had to endure a great amount of emotional pain and shame.

The funny thing about this story is that I could find peace before the provision came when I got my beliefs straight and followed through on what I had been hearing from God. When I was able to fully rest in the thought that God's promises were true, the provision was just a bonus. I realized that sometimes God's provision comes through steps He asks me to take, and it's imperative to listen to His voice.

The idea that we can hear God's voice and be directly guided by Him is one of the main premises to changing your financial story. There are millions of financial options and decisions that need to be made regularly—how much to save for retirement, what type of car to get, what should the grocery budget be, Roth or regular IRA, college fund or not, etc. The combinations and options are endless. Even committed, well-meaning professionals disagree and can give conflicting

Listening To God

advice. That's why this book isn't about what you should do with your finances. There are already plenty of books about that!

I like to write and work on material at a fabulous local coffee shop called Wired[2], and I run into people working in financial services on a regular basis. Many of them are deeply committed Christians. One in particular is a former pastor. All of them speak enthusiastically about their financial products. The ironic thing is most of them disagree with each other about what type of insurance, investments, etc. are the most important. All of them are successful in what they do and are committed to God, yet they all disagree. This is a perfect example of why it is important to listen to God as you walk out of your financial journey. Different options will be different parts of God's plan for different people. Advisors can support you, but you must know God's financial plan for you. This includes His direction from Scripture, but it goes further than that. It includes listening for and knowing when He is speaking to you directly. Many people feel like this concept is a little crazy, but my story (and many others) rest on this foundation. I want to start by sharing some stories and Scriptural background to illustrate this concept. As a part of changing your story, it is absolutely imperative that you can hear from God. It will allow you to avoid fear or confusion in the steps you will take to become a better steward of God's resources.

---

2. Wired Coffee Bar, 5707 Main Street, Ooltewah, TN

My first story about listening to God can be traced back to a time of crisis in my life. I was raised as a good Christian girl. I never drank; waited for sex until marriage, and married a pastor. I spent a lifetime working to do the right things and follow what I felt were the dictates of Scripture. Despite this, I didn't feel close to God. I felt alone and burdened by my never-ending to-do list. I was naturally attracted to topics about "knowing the will of God" because I was constantly questioning what in the world it was!

As my marriage fell apart, everything else in my life seemed to join in with the crumbling. I was separated from my husband, financially broken (I left with two weeks' worth of clothes and not much else), alone for the first time in my life, and terrified. Despite my denial and clinging to the religious traditions I was raised with, it became clear that the "good girl" foundation I built my life around was not working. Driving down the highway one day, I began screaming at the top of my lungs. All the pressure, fear, and disillusionment burst out in a round of tears, expletives, and sobbing. "I've spent my whole life chasing You and trying to do what You wanted me to do, but I don't feel You! My life is falling apart, and where are You? I'm sick of chasing after You when nothing You have promised is happening in my life. I'm done! If You're there, show up, or I'm done!"

It was the most honest prayer I had ever prayed. Being a "good girl," I was sure that, rather than responding to this temper tantrum, God would keep a disapproving silence at my language and defiance. But instead, for the first time in my life, I felt like I heard God speak directly to me. It was not an audible voice, but just a thought that I knew without a doubt, had not come from me. And as strange as it was, the fact that it was strange was part of how I knew it was God. This was not something I would have ever come up with on my own. In the same way you might spontaneously visualize a conversation with a friend, I saw an image of God smiling at me. He said, "I've been waiting for you to get honest with me." It was a turning point in my life (another one). I wasn't chasing after a fog. I had a real conversation with God. He was not threatened at all by me, or the intensity of my feelings. And beyond that, I got the sense He was gently amused and proud of my passion.

I have come to believe that God loves these prayers. He promises we will find Him when we seek Him with our whole hearts. My heart isn't always butterflies and tulips. It is, at times conflicted, angry, deceptive, selfish, or fearful. When I began to show up with all the pieces of my heart, the good and the bad, God began to speak to me.

You may struggle with this concept or feel this isn't how you've experienced God in the past. God doesn't always work with us in the same way we've experienced in the past. He will have some surprises in store while He finishes the work He promised to do in you.

Scripture also happens to be full of examples of God speaking with people. In Genesis 24, we find Abraham telling us how God spoke to him and called him away from his homeland. In Genesis 16, we find God speaking to Hagar, the cast-off wife who was a symbol, in many ways, of Sarai's lack of faith. In Exodus 6, God talks to Aaron and Moses about leading the Israelites out of Egypt. Later in Exodus 33, Scripture says, "The Lord would speak to Moses, face-to-face, as a man speaks with his friend" (NIV). I Samuel 3 has a vivid picture of God waking Samuel from sleep by calling his name. Samuel thought Eli was calling him from another room! II Samuel 2 talks about David, asking God if he should move. God said yes, and David asks the next logical question: Where? God responds again by directing David to Horeb. As King, David never actually lost a battle because he went into all of them asking God for his literal "marching orders." In I Kings 19, God appears to Elijah, asks him what he's doing there, and tells him where to stand.

We don't know how God speaks to us, other than the direction in I Kings 19, stating God spoke in a still, small voice. Scripture doesn't specify if this was audible, but many current stories of people hearing from God included variations. Some get the impression of a thought, a picture, a dream, and yes, some have heard audible voices. The point is, when we are in a relationship with God, we recognize His voice.

I believe God speaks to us in line with how He created us. Some of you are auditory learners and some of you have vivid imaginations that see things very clearly. In your journey of listening, be on the lookout for it to come in a way that is personal to you. As your relationship deepens, you will learn to recognize how He communicates with you more and more clearly.

In Isaiah 50:4-5, we hear, "The Sovereign Lord has given me an instructed tongue, to know the word that sustains the weary. He wakens me morning by morning, wakens my ear to listen like one being taught." It has been my experience that teachers generally talk quite a bit. Should we expect anything less from God? The next verse is particularly interesting. "The Sovereign Lord has opened my ears, and I have not been rebellious, *I have not drawn back*" (NIV). How many times do we, either consciously or unconsciously, draw back from hearing God because we're scared of what He's going to say? I used to be terrified that if I surrendered or listened to God, He would send me to a mud hut in a far off country…not something I longed for. That isn't how God works. Yes, there are times God asks us to do difficult things to grow us, but He created us. He created us with gifts and longings for fulfillment. I heard a character on *Self-Made: Inspired by the Life of Madam CJ Walker*, say, "Our dreams are God's way of showing us our future."

Some of you may have noticed that most of the examples so far are from the Old Testament. Maybe you think that, when Jesus came, there was no more need for God to speak. Or that Scripture has become more widely distributed, and we can gain all the direction we need from it. Not so.

Try the following examples on for size.

"The man who enters by the gate is the shepherd of his sheep. The watchman opens the gate for him, and the sheep listen to his voice. He calls his own sheep by name and leads them out. When he has brought out all his own, he goes on ahead of them, and his sheep follow him because they *know his voice*" John 10:2-4 (emphasis added). In John 14:26, Jesus says, "But the Counselor, the Holy Spirit, whom the Father will send in my name, will teach you all things and will remind you of everything I have said to you."

A dramatic example of being spoken to is in Acts 9:3-4. Saul (later Paul) is on the way to Damascus. He is blinded, and God asks, "Why are you persecuting me?" A few verses later, God calls a man named Ananias to go to Saul and heal him of his blindness. What follows, in effect, is an argument between Ananias and God because Ananias has heard of Saul's penchant for killing Christians. God continues to confirm what Ananias is to do. In the end, Saul is healed of his blindness and becomes one of the most powerful witnesses for God in the early church.

In Luke 2:26, Scripture talks about Simeon knowing—because it had been revealed to him by the Holy Spirit—that he would not die before he had seen Christ. And finally, at the end of Scripture in Revelation 3:20, God says, "Here I am, I stand at the door and knock. If anyone hears my voice and opens the door, I will come in and eat with him, and he with me."

John Eldredge speaks to this topic in his book, *Walking With God*.

> Now if God doesn't also speak to us, why would He have given us all these stories of Him speaking to others? "Look—here are hundreds of inspiring and hopeful stories about how God spoke to His people in this and that situation. Isn't it amazing? But you can't have that. He doesn't speak like that anymore." That makes no sense at all. Why would God give you a book of exceptions? ... What good would a book of exceptions do you? That's like giving you the owner's manual for a Dodge even though you drive a Mitsubishi. No, the Bible is a book of examples of what it looks like to walk with God. To say that He doesn't offer that to us is just so disheartening. It is also unbiblical.

Don't get caught up in the idea that God doesn't speak outside of Scripture. Hopefully, this chapter has made a strong case for trying what will without a doubt be the most pivotal, powerful, and exciting journey of your life. Why not start now? Write down some questions and start to practice hearing His voice.

When Listening Changes Everything

A few years ago, Marcel and I were sitting in church. Sitting in the row in front of us were a father and his little toddler. The little guy was super out-going, and he turned around to make faces and chatter at us. We smiled and waved, and at the same moment, I saw an image in my mind of another little boy standing next to the child chattering at us. He looked just like my husband, and he was grinning at me, too. In that moment, I knew it was the boy we would have someday. The thought came unbidden, "He will be exceptional." All of this happened in an instant, and although I was startled, there was a certainty in me. I couldn't have argued with it, even if I wanted to. My husband and I had never been sure we would have children. The responsibility scared us, and we were both more focused on career and calling than parenting. At that moment, though, I couldn't wait to meet the precious little boy who looked so much like the man I love. I knew it might take a miracle to get my husband ready to have a child, but I figured that was God's business.

    About two years later, I started to feel I would become pregnant soon. It was a mixture of intuition and logic; knowing my age made the issue a little more urgent. One morning, I was scheduled to speak on faith at a church, I heard God whisper, "Have sex with your husband." Notice He didn't need to suggest I ask my husband, agreement with this plan was a given! This was quite shocking to me, and I was too wound up about speaking. I didn't want to have sex. That whisper continued, though, and I followed through. My husband and I had a wonderful time together, and it turned out to be a really wonderful way to go into a speaking engagement. I felt loved, relaxed, grounded, and confident.

From that place, God really moved in the service, and I was walking on air.

Before church, I began to write a personal script in my head when I realized it was the perfect time of the month for conception. I thought how amazing it was of God to choose the timing when I was speaking on faith. I was quite expectant that this would be the time. A week later, at a women's breakfast, I asked for a fleece from God just to be sure I wasn't getting ahead of myself. During the sermon, I asked God to confirm if I was truly pregnant by having the speaker talk about birth and conception. She was talking about something that had nothing at all to do with procreation, but in the next moment, she began talking about pregnancy. Looking back, I have to admit something still didn't feel certain in my gut, and it certainly wasn't on the level of a sheepskin getting wet while the grass was dry. But a fleece was a fleece, and I began praising God and thinking about how to rearrange the house for a nursery.

What About When We Hear Wrong?

A few days later, my period arrived. I can't say that I've ever really welcomed it with open arms, but that month I was well and truly angry about it. I don't think I could overstate how deeply betrayed I felt; how my faith was shaken. Yes, I was disappointed about not being pregnant, but the core issue was questioning if everything I staked my life on was wrong. I had been so sure about His voice on the matter and being wrong made me question everything I thought I had ever heard from God. Was I just deluding myself to believe He was directing me?

 The week after the women's breakfast, I went to a conference with some friends. On the drive there, they listened as I cried out my struggle and anger. On a phone call the night we arrived, I shared the depth of my anger with my husband. God and I don't hold back in our conversations, but Marcel got upset with me, saying I shouldn't be talking to God the way I was. As a man, he was personally offended by the lack of respect I was exhibiting toward God. I muddled through the days away from home, trying not to be too much of a downer without much success. At the end of the conference, we attended a worship service, and the speaker, Craig Hill, talked about the Israelites and their promised land. I began to mutter under my breath, "Where's my promised land, God? I wasn't even thinking about kids. You brought it up." God responded, "You said you have surrendered everything to me. That means I can have my way with you." My anger spiked higher at that point. The language seemed demeaning, and I pointed that out in my head while Craig Hill went on, unaware of my little drama.

 God proceeded to remind me I had surrendered to Him because I know my heart was (and is) safe with Him. As I thought back on my journey, I begrudgingly acknowledged that was true. In the next few moments, I surrendered again, more deeply than ever before, on a deeper plane than

I knew existed. I surrendered to trust even when I didn't understand. Even if it looked to me like I had been betrayed, somehow it sunk in that I won't be betrayed, and I can rest in that no matter what the situation looks like. A few hours after that service, I anxiously left to get home to Marcel. I was at peace again, and I missed my husband. I wanted to tell Marcel that God and I weren't fighting anymore and share the peace I had experienced from our heart to heart. I felt a happy desperation to hold Marcel and tell him what had happened. That night, we conceived our son.

I have come to believe that if God says it to me, "It Is." I may not see it in the natural world yet, but it is as good as done. Yes, there are possibilities for disappointment in the journey of listening to God, but the benefits and peace outweigh them all.

Here's the thing, I talk face-to-face with my husband daily. Even though I am in his physical presence during most conversations, there are times where I still misunderstand him. At times, this leads to frustration or even heated debate. But I don't stop talking to him! The misunderstandings teach me about who he is. And each time, I come away listening more carefully to him and knowing something deeper about his heart. It is no different in our relationship with God. Don't let disappointments or misunderstandings keep you from seeking His voice. Dig in and sort it out.

How do we avoid misunderstanding God? It's important to note that God told us He is not the author of confusion, nor has He given us a spirit of fear. "For He [who is the source of their prophesying] is not a God of confusion and disorder but of peace and order".[3] "For God did not give us a spirit of timidity (of cowardice, of craven and cringing and fawning fear), but [He has given us a spirit] of power and of love and of a calm and well-balanced mind and discipline and self-control".[4]

If you are working toward making a financial decision and there is fear, confusion, or lack of calm or self-control, you can be assured that it is not God led. Wait until your mind and spirit are calm before making a decision. If you're afraid of missing an opportunity, let it go. God is the source of every resource. When you're ready, He can bring the right opportunity to your doorstep in millions of creative ways. Do not lose your peace jumping in before you are in peace and power.

One of the first investments Marcel and I made was a vending machine. In the grand scheme of things, it was not a huge investment, but it was our first, and when we talked about it, I was nervous. It was more money than we generally spent on one purchase, and there were moments of uncertainty as we looked for a location and researched costs. As we continued to pray and search, the peace always came. By the time we made the purchase, we were excited, and there were no concerns left. If we made the decision before

---

3. I Corinthians 14:33 (AMP)

4. 2 Timothy 1:7 (AMP)

we felt peaceful, we would have spent the next few years second-guessing the decision when we began to get tired of filling it up! We ended up learning a ton about the joy of making an investment and seeing a return on the money and what it looks like to steward an investment.

Another way to refine our hearing and make sure we aren't misunderstanding God is a concept I learned from one of my friends and mentors, Julia Winston. Working with Kingdom business owners, she talks a lot about our authority and impact coming from an internal congruence. She defines this as what happens when our spirit, soul, and body all line up. Another way of describing this is our external, internal, and eternal identities lining up. External identity is how people perceive you, what they notice you're good at, and what your eccentricities are—the things that make you uniquely you. Internal identity is how you see yourself and the things you tell yourself about who you are. Eternal identity is who God created you to be! As you can probably imagine, when all three of those things are lined up, you are going to be walking in a lot of certainty, power, and authority. These three aspects can also be a powerful listening tool. Have you ever been talking to God about something, and a thought comes that you aren't sure about? The question comes to mind, "Was that my idea, or God's?" One way to measure that is to check in with those three parts of yourself. How does your spirit feel about it? How does your intellect feel about it? How does your soul or your emotions feel about it? If you aren't on the same page with all 3 of those areas, take the time to talk it through with God and figure out where the hang-ups or obstacles are. I believe this is a way to avoid the double-mindedness that James talks about in the first chapter. This is also a good way to make sure you're hearing from God clearly.

Those Pesky Agreements

We talked earlier about the agreements we make that we feel are based on facts and how it is vital to make sure the agreements you hold in your heart line up with Scripture. If they don't, they aren't accurate and will get in the way of you hearing accurately. Here's another example of how this works. If I believe someone to be evil, even if they say something kind to me or do something that seems to be in my best interest, I won't receive it. I will not believe that what they are doing is truly good for me and I will reject it. It is no different from our relationship with God.

How to Listen

Now that we're clear on the reality and importance of God's voice in your life, how do you learn to hear Him? The following are a few ideas:
- Make a list of agreements/beliefs you have about your finances and make sure they line up with Scripture. (Feel free to refer back to the chapter on beliefs for support on this.) If they don't, ask God to heal those prior to making big financial decisions. If the financial decision has to be made quick-

ly, don't forget God knows the answer. He can change your heart in a moment. Talk to Him and listen for the solutions. Ask Him to heal those agreements through the situation you're in.

•Practice listening! Ask God questions, either about things on your heart or questions you have about Scripture. You can even ask God what to talk about! Sit in the silence afterward, and see what comes to mind. You may even practice writing down your questions and writing what comes to mind afterward. This helps you to track and confirm what you're hearing. Keep in mind the ways you feel most connected to God as well. And expect to listen and hear in that way. For example, I follow many Kingdom-minded business people, and one guy I respect a great deal talked about the need to be outside in order to hear from God. He suggested going for a walk to gain strategies and guidance for business. I thought this sounded like a reasonable idea, so I set out the next morning for a walk. Right out of the gate, I walked through a spider's web and spent the next ten minutes trying to get the last sticky pieces out of my mouth and nose. I began to sweat from the accursed humidity (the South is known for it), and somehow started sneezing while I made a concerted effort not to trip over the roots and rocks on the trail. It occurred to me that this was not the best way for me to connect with God! I tried a few more days to be sure. After that, I quickly went back to quiet mornings snuggled in my robe with a pen and hot tea. Yup, there was that quiet voice again! You are fearfully and wonderfully made, unlike anyone else on the planet. Allow yourself the honor of connecting in the unique ways that God designed you.

•Confirm what you sense/hear with Scripture. I know a man who left his wife for another woman and told people that God had guided him to the other woman. God will never ask you to do something that disagrees with the principles of His word. Faulty agreements or pain from the past have the power to confuse our understanding of what we hear. As you learn to listen, you can check and confirm what you hear by the standard of Scripture. You may also find that there are times that God will whisper something that totally blows your mind. He may say something that disagrees with what you've always been taught or assumed the Bible teaches. These are especially fun moments because we can find a completely new paradigm in a moment!

•Be persistent. I have always gotten a kick out of the idea that God doesn't mind when we "harass" Him. Luke 18 talks about a judge who wasn't a believer and didn't care about justice. A widow was in a battle with an adversary and asked the judge for help. He ignored her, but she kept coming after him. Finally, he gave her the support she needed, not because he changed his mind or cared for her. He did it simply to get her off his back. The great news about this story is that God cares a great deal about supporting you. (This story may even have just uncovered an agreement of yours that doesn't line up with Scripture. How many of you feel like God is like the judge who doesn't care and just wants you off His back?) God has promised to be a shield for you. Later in the story, God says, "Will not God give justice to His elect who cry to Him day and night? Will he delay long over them? I tell you, he will give justice to them speedily."[5] When you are persistent in your prayers, He takes note. As you persist in practicing hearing from Him, you will hear more clearly.

•Confirm what you believe you're hearing with a mature believer. It is important to note that legalists are not mature believers. They may look like it at first glance because they are usually very focused on their image and looking just right. But people in this phase of their walk with Christ are all about performance and duty. They often find listening to God to be a threat to their plans. You will need to make sure you ask for confirmation from a believer with their own dynamic walk with God and hears His voice in their own lives. The fruits of the spirit will be very obvious and active in them.[6]

•Ask for a fleece. A fleece is basically a safeguard. When you feel like you're getting some direction from God, you can ask Him to confirm with a sign (You can read about Gideon and the original fleece in Judges 6). I like to ask for a fleece when I hear something, and the stakes are very high. When Gideon asked for a fleece, God had asked him to lead men into battle. Gideon didn't think very highly of himself, and even though he was willing to obey God, he wanted to be very sure his signals weren't crossed!

---

5. Luke 18:1-8 (ESV)

6. Galatians 5:22

- As you continue reading this book, begin to ask God questions and listen for His leading about the concepts you are learning. Ask if this or that concept applies to you and how God wants to interact with you on them. If something that's written challenges your beliefs or you feel confused, use that as an opportunity to talk and listen to God. Have fun with it! You will find this journey to be exciting and full of adventure. Just think about it, God knit you together with dreams, talents, and vision. He designed you for something. As you listen to Him, He will reveal more and more aspects of His plan for your life, and you will find yourself living with confidence and peace you may not have thought possible. The shame and fear most of us have learned to take for granted is not God's plan for you.

Chapter 3
Fear

By being vulnerable, you become invulnerable.

Fear is rampant in our culture. About 80% of what people reported as their main concern in my private practice was anxiety. I would bet a good bit of money that those who have dreamed or tried and failed to launch a business have gotten even more up close and personal with fear. As a friend of mine and fellow entrepreneur has said, "You want to find out what all your issues are? Start a business." It has a knack for bringing up known and unknown insecurities! And ladies, I used to fear everything. Tests, failure, getting fat, getting old, not being wanted (which was guaranteed to fail because honestly, I wanted every man I knew to fall at my feet), not having enough money, having too much money (because that was sinful, you know), not being the best… at everything, etc. All the anxiety kept me from one of my fears…I never gained weight because all that worry kept my stomach tied up in knots. It was a miserable way to live. Many years later, starting a business brought up fears I hadn't experienced before.

The majority of people have just come to accept that fear is normal. After all, there seems to be a lot of reasons to fear in our culture these days. Most people have just accepted fear as normal and impossible to live without. Many try to mute the pain by taking prescriptions or using alcohol, drowning in television or sugar. We have a million ways to try to cope. This is a particular soapbox for me because even in the church, it seems that we've just accepted fear as a way of life. "Feel the fear and do it anyway," we say. How would it change your life, though, to seek God and bathe in His presence until there was no fear? How would it feel to then move forward in power?! What if the incredibly good—yet hard to believe—news was that fear is only a spiritual issue, and if dealt with spiritually, you need never mess with it again? In tackling this topic, what you believe is, again, extremely vital. If you believe fear is inevitable, you won't ever escape it. So let's dive in and talk about this some more.

No book on finances is balanced without a look at how fear impacts us. Books on finances often give us techniques to manage our money, but fear can block us from productively using the techniques. Many of us grew up without any solid information on managing finances. Beyond that, fear made us do a myriad of crazy and sometimes downright ridiculous things in our relationship with money. As believers, we are actually promised something completely different than fear. "You will guard him and keep him in perfect constant peace (aka *shalom*) whose mind [both its inclination and its character] is stayed on You and hopes confidently in You[1]".

The original language of peace in this verse is "*shalom*, and, according to Strong's Concordance, *shalom* means "completeness, wholeness, health, peace, welfare, safety, soundness, tranquility, prosperity, perfectness, fullness, rest, harmony, the absence of agitation or discord." *Shalom* comes from a root meaning to be complete, perfect, and full. This is what we are promised as believers, and it is very different than the fear many have come to expect. This chapter will address the issue of fear in changing your financial stories and allow you to live the *shalom* intended for you.

What is fear exactly? The dictionary[2] defines it as "an unpleasant emotion caused by the belief that someone or something is dangerous, likely to cause pain, or a threat." As someone who came from a long line of people who struggled mightily with anxiety, that sounds way too detached for me. Fear was a stomach constantly tied up into knots; it was waking up in the middle of the night, terrified of being alone, failure, or having enough money. It was resentment toward people who seemed confident or didn't have my worries. It was a crushing unknown. But overall, it was something I felt completely and utterly powerless to. Maybe you relate. Scripture talks about us not being given a spirit of fear[3]. This can

---

1. Isaiah 26:3 (AMP)
2. www.dictionary.com
3. 2 Timothy 1:7

be a disposition. But in the original language of the verse, it can actually be an unclean spirit or a demon. I'm not calling you demon-possessed. I don't think I was, and I certainly was fearful…about something…almost all the time. So even if that concept is hard to swallow, the really good news is that fear is not one of the fruits of the spirit[4] and doesn't ever come from God. If you are feeling fear, you are under satanic attack, and that, my dear, means you are important and strategic in this battle for kingdom.

    There is an educational company doing a great deal of work educating individuals about finances and business. They are fond of saying, "the roots create the fruits.[5]" I will never forget hearing the testimony of one of their very wealthy executives. Once, he shared about his abusive childhood and how his father regularly told him he wouldn't amount to anything. This message was usually drilled in by a physical beating. Understandably, this young man grew up harboring a lot of anger and fear. It was the basis for his drive to prove his father wrong. The wealthy executive shared how he became very successful. The more money the man made, the angrier (and more fearful) he got. This was when he shared that money makes people more of what they already are.

    He was angry and scared at his core, and the more money he made, the more anger and fear he experienced. So

---

4. Galatians 5:22

5. Peak Potentials

the question is, do you like who you are? Do you want to be more of it? Part of changing your financial story is to make your heart ready so that when you become "more" of what you are now, it is a gift rather than a curse. This executive's story changed when he dealt with his core feelings toward his father. When he forgave. My story changed when I dealt with my fears around money and forgave myself for the mistakes I had made.

As I've mentioned earlier, for most of my life, the fear felt all-encompassing. I was frustrated because I had no idea how to escape it. At one point, a friend asked me, "What were you afraid of?" I wasn't even sure at times. But in general, I was afraid of being abandoned without resources. I was afraid of not keeping my word in paying bills, but the core of my problem with finances stemmed from my lack of belief in God's provision. I didn't believe I had or would have the funds I needed to pursue the dreams in my heart. And for me, there wasn't anything more horrifying than not being able to do what I ached to do.

Today, I'm aware. All the things I feared were lies from Satan, but as long as I believed them, I was absolutely powerless against fear. Money had become a God to me, even though I wasn't aware of it consciously. Satan figured out it was an effective trigger for me and used it regularly. From a practical perspective, how this played out in my life was that I would panic when I felt I didn't have any money. I generally began to spend money to subconsciously prove to myself that I could supply what I needed or wanted. My belief was that God wouldn't supply what I needed, and debt would do what God wouldn't.

This set up a trend for debt that plagued me most of my adult life. At one point, I was reading some old journals I'd written ten years before and realized I was still struggling with the same issues of fear as I had back then! This made me angry. My response was to ask God to clear the issue once and for all. It was a full and almost defiant surrender. The gloves came off! I had come far enough to realize life wasn't meant to be lived like this. I was full of almost constant fear, but Scripture was full of admonishments not to fear.

In fact, the only thing we are instructed to fear is God. Now for those of you who have rigid religious upbringings, please note that the fear spoken of in Scripture in the original language is yare, and it is an awe and reverence for God. We're meant to have a healthy respect for the Father, knowing who He is and what He has done. Throughout the Old Testament, the Israelites are told in numerous life-threatening situations not to fear; God was with them.

"Have I not commanded you? Be strong and courageous. Do not be afraid; do not be discouraged, for the Lord your God will be with you wherever you go" (Joshua 1:9, NIV). In Exodus 20:20, Moses says to the people, "Fear not; for God has come to prove you, so that the [reverential fear

Fear

of Him may be before you, that you may not sin." 2 Timothy 1:7 is especially encouraging. It says, "For God did not give us a spirit of timidity (of cowardice, of craven and cringing and fawning fear), but [He has given us a spirit] or power and of love and of calm and well-balanced mind and discipline and self-control.[6]

God came through in every situation, and He did it despite their poor attitudes. It is also encouraging because, based on these verses, we know that if we are in fear, we are under spiritual attack. Fearful feelings aren't from God. At the same time, for much of my life, verses like this made me feel automatically guilty. I didn't know how *not* to be afraid. John 14:2 (AMPC) was a puzzle to me. "Peace I leave with you; My [own] peace I now give and bequeath to you. Not as the world gives do I give to you. Do not let your hearts be troubled, neither let them be afraid. [Stop allowing yourselves to be agitated and disturbed; and do not permit yourselves to be fearful and intimidated and cowardly and unsettled.]" Why would God tell me He gave me peace and then tell me not to worry? I always felt that, if I had peace, I wouldn't worry!!

Joyce Meyer speaks to this in her book, *Battlefield of the Mind*,

> Peace is not something that can be put on a person; it is a fruit of the Spirit (see Galatians 5:22), and fruit

---
[6]. Deuteronomy 31:6 (AMP)

is the result of abiding in Jesus (See John 15:4, KJV). Abiding relates to the "rest of God" spoken in the fourth chapter of Hebrews as well as other places in the word of God. Jesus gave us His peace (See John 14:27), but He said we must not allow ourselves to be fearful, intimidated, and unsettled. In other words, peace is present in us, but it must be chosen over what our fleshly mind thinks. We can choose to be peaceful by choosing to think on things that promote peace rather than things that open a door for worry and anxiety. [7]

Our choice comes in what we choose to think about. I once heard a man share in a 12-step meeting, "My mind is a dangerous place, I try not to go in there alone." Not every thought you have is true, and sometimes our minds can be the biggest part of our problems. I have had many clients who struggle with depression and fear. When they begin to share feelings they experience and the self-hatred they have, it is no wonder they're miserable. It is impossible to constantly berate yourself or spend your time thinking about everything that can go wrong and not feel miserable.

I mentioned earlier that Satan is the father of lies. This is one of the saddest ironies and relates to what we've talked about regarding beliefs. I had a client I worked with for many years. She struggled with an eating disorder and chronic, intense anxiety. She was adorable, intelligent, fun-

---

7. Joyce Meyer, Battlefield of the Mind

ny, compassionate, inquisitive, witty, and had a killer work ethic. This woman was also naturally good with money. She wasn't able to see any of that. She saw her disorder, her fear, her failures. Because of what she focused on, she wasn't able to see the gifts. Satan whispered lies in her ears almost constantly. She believed them, and the result was he wrapped her in fear and kept the immense gifts she had from impacting the world. My client is not alone. Satan's technique is the same for all of us. He hasn't had to change it because it has worked for thousands of years, resulting in fear and bondage. This is why Scripture encourages us to think about positive things. It doesn't mean we ignore the pain in the world, but it does mean we learn to look at things from the perspective of God's truth and the hope and power He offers us.

Think about it like this. Do you like the results you currently have around finances in your life? If not, trace back to your thoughts. Your thoughts create your feelings (either positive or negative). Feelings then dictate your actions, and actions lead to your results. If you don't like your results, go back to your thoughts (your roots) and adjust them.

There is something I need to note before we go on. You may feel like you are very careful about your thoughts already, but you're still not getting the results of Scripture promises. If that is the case, you are likely dealing with subconscious thoughts. These thoughts are more powerful at driving us than our waking thoughts, and they are hard to identify at times because they are well…subconscious! They are outside our awareness, and we aren't actively aware of having them. This is something you can ask the Holy Spirit to help you identify and if you feel led, look into some of the Change Your $tory workshops or one of the online programs.

The most powerful way of adjusting your thoughts will be to go to Scripture and start claiming the truths listed there. When you come to promises you can't believe are true, ask God to heal your heart and help you to see the truth in them. This goes back to what we discussed earlier about not lying to yourself because of the stress it causes the body.

To start with, do a study of what the Bible says about finances, write down texts that speak to you particularly, and dive deeper into understanding the texts that don't initially make sense to you (www.biblestudytools.com is an excellent free resource to help with this). Begin to claim the truths when you have a thought that doesn't line up or when you have a thought you know is leading to bad results. It is the Holy Spirit's job to heal your roots, and it will happen quickly when you begin to make a conscious choice to line up your thoughts with the truth in Scripture.

Chapter 4
Shame

---

*Somewhere in the world, there is a darkness only you can heal.
To do it, you have to face your own.*

A young man gains an inheritance when his parents die, and a few months later, it's gone. A young woman gets a credit card in college, and 15 years later, she is still paying it off. A single parent racks up debt trying to keep their child from going without. The thing all of these individuals have in common is **shame**. All of them know that the choices they made are costing them dearly, and most of them have probably heard Dave Ramsey or Suze Orman talk about how bad these decisions are. Fear tells them there isn't any other way, and shame puts the last nail in the coffin by saying they don't deserve a way out, even if there was one.

There are many ways to describe shame. One description is "the fear of being known," because shame innately hides. In the description above, the thing all these people have in common is a deep fear of people knowing about the money choices they've made. But this succinct description doesn't capture the essence of this thing hiding in darkness, tripping us up repeatedly. You might find some shame hiding (or maybe not hidden at all) when you think of how you perceive yourself with money. My experience has been that clients prefer to talk to me about extramarital affairs, abuse, politics, anything other than finances. Often the reason for that is shame. Shame over what they don't have, what they do have, how they handle it, how they got it, etc. What thoughts come to mind when you think of money? Often people will say, "I'm not good with money." The core of that statement is shame. You'll find that most of the beliefs you have that don't line up with Scripture have shame at their root.

Shame is the voice that whispers directly the opposite of who and what God created you to be. It is insidious because part of what shame whispers is often the truth. Shame used to whisper to me that I couldn't help women heal their hurts around money because I was a horrible money manager. There was some truth to that! But that whisper is what was true of me without the power of the Holy Spirit guiding me. It is the truth of who we are when we aren't abiding in the vine.[1] When I learned to abide in the vine around that particular half-truth, I realized there are people God designed to manage money, and they were thrilled to help me manage mine! I could help women deal with the core issues, and I could bring in people to help myself and my clients learn how to manage it now that we weren't scared of it! At its core, shame is about incorrect identity. The only way out of shame is the kingdom route.

---

1. John 15:5

In Scripture, Jesus talks about ignoring the shame He felt to focus on the joy set before Him.[2] I imagine there was intense joy in knowing what He went through saved the people He loved. Strong's Concordance tells us that the meaning of the original language for shame in this text is: "The feelings that leads one to shun what is unworthy out of a prospective anticipation of dishonor." Jesus hated the shame He felt when He took on the sins of the world. Imagine the darkest secrets you carry, and now imagine feeling this weight for everyone who has ever lived. Jesus understands shame, and He was willing to push through it to face the joy on the other side that waited for Him and us. Our shame is no different. When we face it and push through, joy waits for us on the other side. That is why addressing shame about our relationship with finances is so vital. If you feel shame regarding your relationship with money, you will naturally shun it. We will do almost anything to avoid dishonor, even if we are the only ones who know about it!

Joyce Meyer has her own take on shame in her book, *The Battlefield of the Mind*. She talks about Joshua 5:9, "And the Lord said to Joshua, this day I have rolled away the reproach of Egypt from you…" The word reproach means "blame…disgrace: shame." God was telling Joshua that He was going to roll away the shame from the Israelites. God's plan for you, financially or otherwise, includes rolling away your shame.

---

2. Hebrews 12:2

This chapter is also what makes the Change Your $tory material fundamentally different from other programs. I'm pretty sure most of you have been introduced to the idea that your mindset is important to your success. Many of you may already agree that listening for spiritual direction is vital. But have you ever had anyone talk to you about financial shame and how getting rid of it can launch you into your dreams and calling? I find myself wishing we were sitting in a living room somewhere, curled up in a comfy chair, talking about this! Clearing shame was a game-changer for me. It made me unashamed to pursue my dreams even when it was a long journey, and others thought I was crazy. So pay close attention, ladies! Freedom is close by!

Healthy vs. Toxic Shame

Some of you may think that shame isn't such a bad thing, and there are times when it has an appropriate role to play. Even among professionals in my field, there is some controversy around this topic. Some professionals say that shame can lead to good things depending on our response to it. Trying to figure out the difference between healthy vs. toxic shame can be confusing though. It can take a bit of mental gymnastics. Annibale Pocaterra, one of the first individuals to write about shame, sees shame as our teacher (a horrible and ineffective teacher if you ask me). According to him, our feelings are innate and are only good or bad, depending on how they're used.[3] Example: a person feels ashamed because

---

3. James Bradshaw, Healing The Shame That Binds You

Shame

of bouncing a check or making a bad investment. That leads them to be more careful or use another more effective system. According to him, this can be termed healthy shame because it led to healing and improvement. I would suggest that looking at shame this way can be sacrificing God's best for the earth's system of getting by. In the same way fear shouldn't be accepted as normal and necessary, shame is a spiritual lie designed to keep you from being who God designed you to be.

I propose we replace the terms "healthy shame" with a different word…humility. If you look up this word, you'll find many different definitions. For our purposes, I love the one in the *Urban Dictionary*.

> True humility is to recognize your value and the value of others while looking up. It is to see there is far greater in us that we can become, who others can become, and how much more we can do or be. To be humble is to serve others and be for their good as well as your own. To be humble is to have a realistic appreciation of your great strengths, but also of your weaknesses." Humility says, "I messed up and didn't pay attention to my balance, I better look at another system to track things."

Toxic shame regarding the bank balance problem would say, "You're no good with finances," which could lead to an ongoing avoidance of the checkbook and more bounced checks. Shame leads us to hide and tells us we are faulty at our core. How many of you reading this book continue to stay in financial patterns causing devastating consequences? Meanwhile, shame has whispered in your ear that you aren't capable of doing things differently. Or maybe you do just fine at managing your daily financial life, but you know the job you're in isn't your calling. You stay in that job though because you don't believe you can go for your dreams because of money. You feel ashamed of what you don't have and ashamed that fear has kept you from moving forward. In contrast, our humility tells us we made a mistake and allows us to get support to do things differently. Humility allows us to admit our struggle and get help from someone capable of helping us. Humility allows us to make mistakes and to be human. Humility is kingdom. "Healthy shame" is the earth system's way of trying to dress up something the enemy intends to destroy you.

In my family system growing up, humility was an emphasized concept, but I didn't like it much. I saw humility as synonymous with weakness and getting stepped on. Early in my 20's when I began my recovery journey, I listened to a program that defined humility as "power under control." It was a huge shift for me, and I became attracted to that concept! Dr. Jordan Peterson, a University of Toronto Professor of Psychology, says the word "meek" (as used in the Bible) is derived from the Greek version of the Bible. Many of the early versions were written in Greek. Being meek at that time meant people who had weapons, like swords, and could use them, but were determined to keep them sheathed. Through this act of humility, they remained in the proper moral position. So, it actually means a moral high ground that is maintained when someone has the ability to use force but doesn't.[4] Those of you who struggle to get a handle on your money, who have attempted to launch your dreams and failed—humility means all of those attempts you made have been valuable learning lessons. Humility means you have weapons, and you know how to use them! It means when you deal with your shame and heal it, when you turn to God in humility, He arms you for battle and prepares you to fight His way. Fighting His way means you win!

Richard Bandler, one of the founders of neurolinguistic programming, also has an interesting take on what he terms healthy shame (that we know is humility!). He believes that a lack of humility limits creativity. If we know we are right, we stop searching for other options and solutions. If you assume you know everything there is to know about managing money, or if you believe having money is wrong, you won't look for other options.

Lastly, and maybe most importantly to the human experience, humility promotes intimacy. Have you ever been in a relationship with someone nice and personable, but they've never shared a single detail about who they are or what they struggle with? It's likely you don't feel connected to them at

---

4. https://steemit.com/philosophy/@annhoyblog/power-under-control-is-the-true-meaning-of-meekness

all. Intimacy requires that we see into each other, viewing the vulnerabilities behind the mask, and bringing those into the relationship. My old therapist, Jeff Seat, used to say, "Intimacy is 'into me, see.'" When I am humble enough to let you see behind my masks, we find out we aren't all that different. By being humble and intimate, thereby being vulnerable, we become invulnerable.

There is a story in the Bible that is one of the most amazing stories about humility and shame not sticking. As the story goes, King David had come back successfully from battle and was leaping about in a way that embarrassed his wife Michal. She came out in a strong attempt to heap some toxic shame on David. "…his wife Michal, daughter of Saul, came out to meet David and said, 'See how the King of Israel has distinguished himself today, going around half-naked in full view of the slave girls of his servants as any vulgar fellow would!'"[5]

Apparently, David had gotten a little exuberant in his dancing and had stripped down to his drawers. Various commentaries tell us that, in the culture of the time, David may as well have been naked. Michal was especially frustrated because it was the tradition of the time to have conquering armies force prisoners to strip and dance as a way of humiliating them. David was so excited about what God had done that he was dancing for joy, fully humbling himself. Rather than taking on the shame she dished out, he responded in this way:

---

5. 2 Samuel 6:20

"It was before the Lord, who chose me above your father (ouch!) and all his house to appoint me as prince over Israel, the people of the Lord. Therefore, I will make merry before the Lord. I will still be more lightly esteemed than this and will humble and lower myself in my own sight. But by the maid you mentioned, I will be held in honor".[6]

David refuted toxic shame by standing in the truth of who God said he was. He had his beliefs straight. Because he didn't make any agreement with the shame she tried to place on him, he was able to remain joyful. The shame she tried to heap on him rolled off his back.

Let's take a closer look at what toxic shame looks like. James Bradshaw wrote the book *Healing the Shame That Binds You*, and he describes the core problem with toxic shame beautifully. "To be shame bound means that whenever you feel any feeling, need or drive, you immediately feel ashamed." Consider your feelings for the next week when the topic of money, investing, etc. comes up. What do you feel? If you *feel* ashamed, you are dealing with toxic shame in this area.

Toxic shame always leads to feeling the need to put on a false front. You may consider that the next time you see a welfare mom in the check-out line with a Coach purse. Or perhaps when your arrogant boss turns red and starts attack-

---

6. 2 Samuel 6:21-22

ing instead of acknowledging a mistake. Both behaviors are masking a painful core of shame. Lashing out at the behaviors that come from a core of shame will only deepen the shame and cause the individual to become more committed to masking it.

There is another incredible story about healing toxic shame in the Bible. I bet you never knew the Bible dealt with shame so well! Most of you may have heard of the woman who had been bleeding for twelve years and forced her way through the crowds around Jesus to touch the hem of his garment.[7] Some of you may not know, in the culture of that time, a woman who was bleeding was considered unclean. If anyone touched her, they had to go through elaborate cleansing rituals. This woman had likely not been physically touched in twelve years (except for the doctors who hadn't been able to help her). Some historians think the bleeding was due to an STD. According to the cultural norms, she was supposed to yell out "unclean" when traveling in crowds so they could avoid her. Talk about intense shame! It is no wonder she tried to sneak through the crowd to try to touch the hem of Jesus' garment.

What happened next may seem cruel to us at first glance. It would be our natural inclination to let the touch go, knowing that someone didn't want to be seen. But Jesus knows the touch of faith and felt the power of it. He also knew the secret to healing shame: It must be brought into the

---

7. Luke 8:43-48

Shame

light. Jesus stopped and forced the woman to tell her story in the middle of the crowd. He didn't just heal her physically. He healed her shame. Sit in that a minute. God isn't aiming to heal you a little bit. He plans to heal everything.

Toxic shame also leads to a loss of self. I would virtually guarantee that prior to her healing, this woman's entire focus was on surviving her disease. She couldn't have had any idea who she was or the purpose for which she was created. We cannot know ourselves fully when we are hiding. All our energy must be expended in keeping the secret of our shame. When we do this, it keeps us from being known and thus, deepens the shame.

My husband, Marcel, found a surprising corner where shame was harbored for him. I came home one night, and Marcel was sitting in the dark as our son slept peacefully in his arms. We hadn't been living with my parents for very long and were still in shock that God had allowed our financial situation to become so poor that this step had been necessary. (In hindsight, launching two new businesses with no business experience at all might have also had something to do with it!). Marcel put Joseph in his crib, and we lay down to talk on the bed. He was quiet and different than normal; pensive. As we talked, my husband shared that something big had just happened. He had been talking to God about his struggle with pride. It had shown up in various areas of Marcel's life, and as Scripture states, it had always led to a fall. He focused his prayers on healing from this issue and recognized that moving in with his inlaws was certainly an effective way of dealing with it. There's not much room for pride as a grown adult having to move back in with parents for a season.

I won't ever forget the look on Marcel's face as he shared that God had told him pride wasn't his problem. Shame was. He began to share stories from his childhood about coming to America as an entitled, wealthy young boy and seeing his father struggle to start a new business in a new country. My husband's family went from an estate on the beach in Rio De Janeiro with a live-in maid and stay-at-home mom to sharing a small room with his sister in Los Angeles. The shame resulting from this led to him putting on a mask. He masked his shame with charm, pride and ego, and a focus on looking good at all times.

His toxic shame masqueraded as pride and ego, and with some prayer and searching, God revealed the true issue in a moment. What we thought was a shameful experience, having to move in with my parents due to our financial situation, turned out to be the light that exposed the shame that had kept my husband bound.

Types of Defense Mechanisms

Marcel's defense mechanism was pride and ego. Defense mechanisms are the things that keep us insulated from our shame. One of my defense mechanisms for my shame around money was to go shopping (i.e., compulsive behavior). Oh, the irony! I didn't have any extra money, which would send me into a panic. I would spend money I didn't have, racking up debt and digging the hole deeper to prove I could meet my own needs and wants. Some defense mechanisms you may recognize are numbing out, denial, projection, rage, arrogance, criticism, contempt, patronizing, envy, and people-pleasing. This is only a partial list, and we will not describe all of them. But perhaps you recognize yourself in some of these behaviors.

Let's start with **arrogance**. It's a pretty common occurrence to see this aspect of toxic shame. You may never have considered this to be an aspect of shame, but think about it. When we are truly secure in who we are (our gifts and our flaws), there is no need to be cocky. There is always fear and pain underneath arrogance.

Denial is also pretty common when it comes to addressing money issues. How many times have you completely ignored the balance in your bank account because it was easier not to know? It is way more fun and less stressful, for a little while, to act like there were thousands of dollars available—until the late notices start coming in.

Envy is hard to avoid when you see someone drive by with your dream car. But, it too, is rooted in shame. The message underneath envy is, "I am not enough with what I have right now." **Numbing out** is at the core of a lot of compulsive behaviors. Alcohol, drugs, television, video games, sex…they are all pretty effective ways to medicate pain and numb out. **Projection** may be an unfamiliar term, but it's a pretty simple concept. When you are projecting, you place something you are feeling onto someone else. If your shame is telling you, you are irresponsible for a stupid mistake you made, in the next minute, you might find yourself wanting to scream the same thing at your child who flunked his spelling test.

We all have **ego defense states**, and for short periods, some of them can be helpful. The body naturally goes into a "numbing out" state when it has experienced physical trauma. This allows us to take action and get to safety before the body collapses. The problem develops when toxic shame makes these defensive states almost constant. We are not capable of functioning fully when they are constantly present. In fact, studies show that this constant state of stress leads to disease.

Let's talk biology for a minute. We have a parasympathetic nervous system (PNS) and a sympathetic nervous system (SNS). The PNS is in charge of growth, healing, and maintenance. The SNS is meant to be used in emergency situations and is involved in what you may have heard called the "fight or flight" system. When the SNS kicks into gear, several things happen in the body. Blood flow changes. It doesn't go to the stomach to digest food or to the frontal lobe to help you with creative thinking, like normal. It doesn't have the same flow to the liver or kidneys. The majority of the blood is going to your muscles because your body thinks it will have to fight or run. When you're in a fight or running for your life, it's not the time to digest food, balance electrolytes, or clear toxins from the liver. Shame causes a low-grade fight or flight response in the body. Over time, as you can imagine, the body shuts down normal functions. Due to this prolonged state, the cells become unable to receive the nutrition they need or unload the waste. This has a huge impact on the immune system, and disease is the result. On the other hand, a Stanford study found that "a cell in growth and healing mode (not in fight or flight) is impervious to disease".[8]

Toxic shame makes the defense mechanisms necessary because shame is exactly that — toxic. Research is making connections between cancer and other life-threatening illnesses due to toxic shame stored in the body. When toxic shame is present, we will do anything to avoid it. You must address this issue if you wish to have a healthy relationship with money.

How do we do it? It may sound big, frightening, and overwhelming. The good news is although it may involve emotion, the process is not necessarily complicated. James Bradshaw puts it this way in his book *Healing the Shame That Binds You*:

> There is a need to surrender spiritually. Admit the shame is there and that you have made poor choices to heal from it. This surrendering is the core of the spiritual paradox that tells us we can only win by losing. This is hard for any hard-driving Ameri-

---

[8]. Alexander Lyon, The Healing Code

can. As with most spiritual laws, it is paradoxical. To find one's life, one must lose one's life. This is a literal truism for shame-based people. We must give up our delusional false selves and ego defenses to find the vital and precious core of ourselves. In our neurotic shame lies our vulnerable and sensitive self. We must embrace the darkness to find the light. Hidden in the dark reservoirs of our toxic shame lives our true self.

Another way of putting this—by becoming vulnerable, by allowing God and safe people to see underneath the mask you wear, you will become invulnerable. There is nothing to hide from and you will find your freedom.

Jesus talked about this as well when He said, "What good would it do to get everything you want and lose you, the real you? What could you ever trade your soul for?"[9] The only way out of toxic shame is through the darkness with confession and accountability. 2 Corinthians 4:2 (AMPC) puts it this way:

> We have renounced disgraceful ways (secret thoughts, feelings, desires, and underhandedness, the methods and arts that men hide through shame); we refuse to deal craftily (to practice trickery and cunning) or to adulterate or handle dishonestly the Word of God, but we state the truth openly (clearly and candidly). And so, we commend ourselves in the sight and presence of God to every man's conscience.

---

9. Mark 8:36b

As I said earlier, at one point in my life, I had decided my life wasn't really worth living the way it was. I was going to place top priority on healing. I attended 12-step meetings, therapy, went to treatment, and sought out people who had overcome and were living lives of meaning. One of the tenets in the 12-step meetings states that the only people who can't heal are those who can't be honest. As I attended the meetings, I noticed there seemed to be different levels of honesty. Some people would show up to the meetings and get honest about a relapse. But if they were asked about something they felt vulnerable about, they would, somewhat defensively, report they were "fine."

At that time in my life, I had five roommates in a big old ranch house. My room happened to be the one closest to the kitchen, and one day I got a snack. It was just a few cookies and milk. I realized halfway back to my room I was slinking back from the kitchen hoping nobody would see me. That moment ended up being the beginning of a slide into a relapse for me which had nothing to do with cookies and milk. I had a desire to hide, even though no one in the house would have given a second thought to my snack. Dishonesty about any area, but especially about areas we're ashamed of, literally weakens us. On the other hand, the speed of your healing in any area will match the pace and depth of your openness. Our bodies are not able or meant to carry the weight of shame and dishonesty.

I want you to try an experiment. Find a partner and hold both your arms straight out in front of you, parallel to the floor. Ask your partner to try to push down your arms. Before your partner does this, think about one of two things. One, something true that you have great peace about, and two, something that you feel shame about. (Shame is the biggest lie there is; it tells you that you can't show up fully in the ways God created you without being wounded).

Now, without telling your partner which one you're thinking about, ask them to push down on your arms while you think of one of these thoughts and then the other. I have never demonstrated this exercise with a client where I couldn't decipher when they were thinking of the thing they were ashamed of, based on the lack of strength in their arms. You can also do the same exercise by holding different substances next to the body, even if you can't see what they are. Your body can't hold the strength if the item is toxic. And as I've said previously, shame is toxic.

In your relationship with money, or any area of your life, God wants to bring your shame into the light and heal it. Just like the woman in Scripture, healing from shame can lead to emotional and even physical healing. This may be why God tells us, in James 5:16, to confess our sins to each other so that we may be healed. Confessing our sins, and thus our shame, opens the door to our healing. In the next section, I've included some ways to address your shame, but if the list seems overwhelming, just remember this: Get honest with God and with the safe people He brings into your life. Everything else will fall into place.

How to Heal From Shame

The following list includes some ways to heal from shame if you found this chapter really resonated with you. Another reason to pay close attention to this list is if this chapter made you really uncomfortable. If you had a highly emotional response and weren't sure why, this is another sign that something was triggered in you. Looking at the following list could be the key to changing your financial story and living the purpose and calling God has on your life.

- **Come out of hiding.** Share with others any shame or mistakes you have about money. This can be a trusted friend, a pastor, mentor, or small group. But show up and tell the truth! It is the first and most important step to being free from shame!

- **Surrender your shame to God.** Remember to do this in a way that feels true to how God wired you. Do you need to go for a hike and speak your surrender to God over a beautiful sunset? Write a letter? Paint a picture, or buy a piece of jewelry that symbolizes Him carrying your shame instead of you? However you do this, I would encourage you to speak the surrender out loud as what we speak is powerful.

- **Find a non-shaming person** and ask them to mirror how they see you after you've shared your shame with them. Remember that Scripture teaches us to have boundaries in our lives. "…Do not throw your pearls before hogs, lest they trample upon them with their feet and turn and tear you in pieces" (Matthew 7:6b). Someone who hasn't healed from their own shame may not know how to deal with yours. Your first decision will be to make sure to find someone you feel safe with. Let them know clearly what type of support or feedback you need from them.

•**Engage in a small group** where honest sharing is honored. I found a supportive space to work through some of the disappointments and struggles of being a kingdom entrepreneur at 100X Academy. It was also an incredible community of support and mentoring around business. It has been life-changing. If you don't have a supportive community in mind, I highly recommend looking into this group and considering it as an invaluable resource. Other options may be 12-step meetings, a small group at church, or a small group of business-minded friends who have a desire to grow and heal as well.

•**Recognize your defense mechanisms** and learn to accept that they helped you cope for a time, but you no longer need them. Find Scriptures that will help you cope in new ways.

•**Look to what Scripture says** you are and learn to stand on it when the critical/shaming voices begin. For those of you who grew up in homes or religions where messages about God were shaming or critical, keep this in mind. Until you work through some of those heart issues, you may feel Scripture paints you in a negative way. If you find yourself feeling ashamed when reading Scripture, just trust me on this. For now, the enemy is whispering in your mind to distort the truth. God isn't shaming or condemning. If this is the case for you, practice some of those listening skills you've learned earlier in the book and ask God to speak to you about how He sees you.

•**Get support** and feedback on a practical level. This is vital for dealing with the shaming people in your life. For example, are there people in your life who constantly criticize you? What might it look like to remove those voices from your life or at least make sure you are guarding your heart when you are in contact with them? This is a really important step. We get more of what we listen to, and you will want to take steps to limit or remove shaming voices in your life.

•**Be aware** of situations that might trigger you into old money behaviors and avoid them. When they do happen, make sure to process with Holy Spirit and/or a trusted friend to help you face the emotions first. Then make the decision pertaining to those money choices.

•**Develop a plan** of integrity and action to deal with money mistakes. This plan needs to include relationships with others and active accountability. Jesus was perfect, and He still maintained a relationship with a small group.

•**Spiritually seek** God's financial plan for your life once the shame and wrong beliefs have been addressed. What if God's original plan for you includes great wealth so you can invest in fighting some of the struggles in our world? What would it look like to be able to support sex trafficking victims, build businesses that give back, or be able to invest in a God-sized business idea that just needs someone to believe in it and put start-up money into it? Don't let wrong beliefs about money keep you from God's plan for you!

Beware When Shame Feels Like Fact

One day, when we were well into the wilderness season of our financial journey, Marcel texted me asking if I knew the account for groceries and household expenses was several hundred dollars in the hole. This was an account I was responsible for, and I immediately checked the balance, thinking he had misunderstood something. As I pulled open the account, I realized he was correct, and panic flowed over me in an immediate deluge. I knew we didn't have the money to cover the balance. I also knew that every day the account stayed like that, it would run up more and more fees. I recognized the panicked deluge of fear also included a hefty dose of shame, even though I knew I hadn't spent any money! I said a prayer, recognizing the chance to practice what I preached, and I called the bank. After a little research, I discovered it was not a mistake on my part, but a mistake by a company that put a particular charge through. I called them next, got the issue addressed, and the money was re-posted to our account almost immediately. Despite my very responsible behavior, I realized about an hour later that I was still feeling ashamed! I had done nothing wrong, but the voices in my head were still ripping me apart. "You will always be bad at managing money; even when you're not avoiding it, you screw up. You've got a long way to go when you can't even handle basic bills. You have a lot of nerve writing a book about teaching people spiritual principles around money."

Here's a little secret about shame. Shame can be so powerfully negative because, just like the serpent did with Adam and Eve in the garden, it tells partial truths. I had historically been a horrible money manager. I had historically avoided dealing with even basic bills due to anxiety and shame. Shame can be hard to avoid because your heart will recognize some truth in the dark whispers. But here's the thing, shame talks to you about who you are without God in your life. It talks about who we are without God's power at work in our finances. Shame is used by the king of darkness to keep you in your place, to keep you from fulfilling your kingdom purpose. The only one who benefits from our willingness to focus on (and agree with) our shame, is Satan. So when it feels like shame is true, and you want to give up in any area of your life, remember the power you have in Christ. Not really sure what that power looks like or how to harness it in your life? We'll get into that in the next chapter. You might be shocked at how simple the answer truly is.

Change Your $tory

Chapter 5
Stepping Into Authority With Your Money

You were gifted for something. Find it and do it!

So, that financial peace and power we talked about in the first chapter is God's plan for us? What actually happens in order for us to begin to live the life God has planned for us? How do we get it? These are big questions on which hinge our entire future and calling! The seed of our answer is found in Philippians 3:10 (AMP). "So that I may know Him [experientially, becoming more thoroughly acquainted with Him, understanding the remarkable wonders of His person more completely] and [in the same way experience] the power of His resurrection [which overflow and is active in believers]." Our authority comes from our intimacy with God combined with knowing and believing who He says we are, not who our shame or fear tells us we are. We are refined and meant to grow into this authority on earth. Think of intimacy with God as the fertilizer for the root system of our trees. Authority is that good fruit we want on our tree. None of us escape toxins in our soil on this earth, but there is something that kills off those toxins and grows our fruit/authority. And it was prepared for us before we were even born. Early on in our financial wilderness season, I told a friend, "I feel like I have this huge unlimited trust fund, but I haven't figured out how to access it."

You only need one thing to begin to understand and access your authority. That one thing? It's intimacy with God. Sounds simple, but in a world with endless options for false intimacy, we often don't know what intimacy looks like. We'll talk about that more in just a minute.

Over and over in Scripture, God makes it clear that his desire is for intimacy…period. If you desire good financial fruit and authority, this is your only path. Our working definition of intimacy for the purposes of this book is "into me, see." God already sees into you. He formed you, and He knows every thought and feeling you have. The question is will we open up to Him and show up in it? If we will learn to look into His heart and listen to His whispers, this is where the magic begins.

Sometimes, people have "wait a minute" moments. You begin to think of all the wealthy people you know who have no belief in God or a discernible spiritual life. It is possible to become wealthy by following certain principles and being committed to them, although there are no guarantees. But it is not possible to do it fearlessly while you ride out the roller coaster. Remember my very wealthy friend, who is an atheist? He said, "I'm wealthy, and I have the ulcers to prove it."

And for those of you who still may find yourself mired in religion, maybe you're a regular church-goer, and you strive to be a good person. You don't feel any particular fire for God, but it is something you check off your to-do list. This was never what God wanted. In fact, if going to church is all you thought God wants from you, I would suggest that church has actually blocked you from seeing all that God has for you. God longs for an intimacy so intense there is nothing that over-shadows its value to you. He longs for an intimacy that involves all of you—spirit, soul, and mind. Picture your favorite love story; God wants to be the leading man in it. If you desire fruit in your life, if you desire authority and power around your relationship with money, this is your path. And part of the beautiful thing about this path is it is as specific, beautiful, mind-blowing, and intricate as your own DNA.

If you'll allow me to step onto a soapbox for just a moment, the church is dying! Why? Because, for so many, it has become only a focus on sets of rules and guidelines for behaviors that don't exist in intimacy! How long would you last on a first date with a guy who began it by listing all his requirements and the ways you would need to change to be loved by him? You'd be out the door in a hot second. Ask any unbeliever in your life what their perception is of Christians, and I can virtually guarantee that love is not the first descriptor they'll use. We teach kids how to obey, and we miss teaching them about passionate, soul-shaking love. When they grow up and look for that passion in sex, alcohol, drugs, tv, or pornography, we judge them. Regarding sex, we view that as the most intimate act we can participate in. That's what Jesus' death and sending the Holy Spirit was about. Christ in us. Holy Spirit in us. And just like the shattering glory of an orgasm, we are meant/designed to feel the shattering glory of God's presence. Our authority in Christ comes from our intimacy with Him "in the bedroom." Please hear my heart on this. I'm using lovemaking as a metaphor and don't intend it to be disrespectful in any way. In fact, I believe this is why God created sex. It is meant to be a picture of the intimacy and closeness He wants to have with us.

In the same way intercourse is the most intimate act we can participate in, when that relationship is forced, it is called rape. This end of the spectrum can be the most soul-shattering thing a person can experience. (Ask anyone who has been raped.)

As a therapist, I've seen the results of some of the worst evil people can perpetuate on one another. I have spent my time wrestling with God on why He allows it. I've realized that evil is what is left free reign to flourish when we are outside of a divine relationship. And as much as God desires intimacy with us, He will not fix that need by "raping" us. He will not force us into intimacy with Him. He doesn't force you, and He won't force the person who abused you because they were outside divine relationship with Him. Intimacy is our choice, exactly as it should be. When we turn away from it (or try to get it in a way we were never designed for), desolation is the result.

So what does intimacy look like? Many of you have experienced more desolation or false intimacy than anything else, so let's break it down.

We'll start with Scripture and paint a picture of what healthy intimacy looks like. It's important to note that we don't experience all the things on the list at all times. We'd likely explode from the overload if we did! Just like any relationship, there are ebbs and flows, but ALL of the upcoming aspects are included in intimacy. One of the ways Christianity has fallen short is when someone is angry or hurting, we tell them to smile or praise (such a pet peeve of mine!). Praise is a facet of intimacy, but so is grieving and anger! Telling someone to smile or praise when they need to curl up and sob in God's lap is abusive and kills intimacy.

Facets of Intimacy:

- **Being one**

- **Grieving** (generally, we don't grieve in front of someone we aren't intimate with)

- **Knowing God** *experientially* and understanding the remarkable wonders of who He is[1]. This means you have actual experiences where you know He led you a certain way, intervened for you, spoke to you, etc. You have *experienced* Him. People without these experiences and interactions tend to struggle with the concept of God. but once you've

---

1. Philippians 3:10

experienced Him, it tends to erase doubts. It also means we have wrestled with God because at times, our experiences lead us to conflict. If you haven't wrestled with God, I would encourage you to do some soul searching and ask Him if you are in *religion* more than a *relationship*. I've known atheists who've wrestled with God more than Christians who aren't passionate enough to lean in. If you are in religion more than a relationship, you may build wealth by using sound principles, but you won't get there worry-free. There may be fear, resentment, confusion, or disappointment when you have a checklist you live up to vs. responding to an intimate, passionate relationship with someone you trust completely. Everything is trash compared to knowing Christ. Keeping a list of rules is inferior. I have come a long way in my walk with Christ, but let's face it, there are a lot of rules in the Bible. Even though I've come to be in a relationship with Him that I'm very passionate about, I still struggled with the idea of intimacy with God. If He truly wanted a relationship, why the seemingly endless lists of rules? In the New Testament, Christ said all of the law (the rules!) was summed up in love. Yes, He wants wholeness for us, but He takes on the responsibility for that. He will write the law on our hearts[2]. That's another way of saying that we will come to experience it. When you see a "rule" in the Bible you aren't practicing, a standard that you can't reach, lean in. Your response can be, "What is your plan for this God? I'm here, do Your thing!"

---

2. Hebrews 10:16

- **Love Him** with everything in us[3]. This doesn't mean that we fake it. It means we get intimate with Him. When we do this, the natural outcome is we begin to love Him with everything in us! The very fact that we sometimes do stupid things when we fall in love with someone is an indicator that we were designed to love fully and passionately. Yet, we make the mistake of believing the unstoppable ache we have is for the person in front of us. No human being is safe to love fully unless we have the foundation of the Father's love. The ache is fulfilled in God, and the person in front of you is the icing on the cake, a gift to show you even more facets of how God loves you.

- **Remain in Him** and He in you[4]. Fruit comes from intimacy. Apart from the vital union, there isn't any fruit, and with Him, nothing is impossible. The word abide means to "sojourn, tarry, to be held, kept, to continue to be present." How does this work? I am still growing in my ability to be fully present or abiding with God at all times, and yet I still walk, eat, etc. I do *something*. I know I don't do it outside of His grace, but it seems to conflict with this text. What does "nothing" really mean in this context? John Gill's Exposition of the Bible specifies that we aren't able to do anything spiritually good. We can work without God but bearing fruit as a natural process comes from abiding (intimacy). This is where our fearlessness comes from. What plant ever got scared about how to bear fruit? It happens without conscious

---

3. Deuteronomy 6:5

4. John 15:4-6

thought when we are abiding. The same as my son grew in my womb after abiding with my husband! I felt the effects of it, but it happened outside my conscious effort.

- **Being a light** for His glory[5]. Manifesting God's glory makes some part of His character visible through us by being what He meant us to be. The original language for God's glory is *kavedh*. The meaning of this word tells us that God's glory is how He makes Himself known and recognizable. Like intimacy, it can have many facets. We all tend to think that the facet most meaningful to us is the "right one," but here are a few examples of God's glory in several different facets. A sunrise or a rainstorm, serving and connecting with someone on a heart level, good food, running, shopping (you know you feel like getting a good deal on something you really love is a spiritual experience!), working on a bike or a car, someone "falling out" in a service. I've felt God's glory watching movies that suddenly connected with my life in such a powerful way that it brought me to tears. I've felt His glory when Scripture hits something deep in my heart, when I'm crying in His arms, when I'm angry at Him and still feel His unwavering love for me. We feel it in music, dancing, or playing, fully present with our children.

- **Wrath**[6]. This one is touchy because so many of us have been harmed by someone shaming or abusing us in the name of "the wrath of God." Fear does motivate for a time, so human

---

5. I Corinthians 10:31

6. Romans 1:18

beings try to use it. But it never lasts, and it never engenders love. Let's take a look at this more closely. "For the wrath of God is revealed from heaven against all ungodliness and unrighteousness of men who by their unrighteousness suppress the truth." The wrath is towards the stuff that suppresses truth and harms us. The wrath can live alongside love, but it's never separated from the love. How do you feel when someone you love deeply betrays you? Wrathful perhaps? The depth of the emotion springs from the depth of your love. You and I tend to take the wrath and run with it, but God never interacts with it or us outside of the context of love. I think it's incredible that God knows the truth will set us free from our shame and fear, so anything that suppresses truth elicits wrath from Him. He gets angry at anything that gets in the way of our freedom.

- **God constantly knocks** and pursues[7].

- **Eats with me** and restores me[8]. Girls, I love this one. Marcel calls me a foodie queen because I have a deep appreciation and enjoyment of good food. Have you ever noticed that there are some people you can't eat with? Your stomach balls up in knots? I dated a guy, very briefly, and he ended up ghosting me. I should have known it was coming because every time I had a meal with him, my stomach was in agony. Something in my spirit knew this relationship wasn't a good idea, even if my conscience was quite invested in dating him.

---

7. Revelation 3:20
8. Psalms 23

On the other hand, picture the man of your dreams eating your favorite meal with you. Maybe you are grabbing tidbits off of each other's plates. Laughing as you roll your eyes in ecstasy over a particularly fabulous bite. He's beautiful and strong, and you know he'll protect you with all His passion and power. You are safe. A simple meal restores you.

- **Our soul longs for Him**[9]. We tend to think it is a longing for other things…that man, that car, that career, that income, that baby, that tv show, that purse, that drink, that high, that orgasm…It's not those things, it's Him we crave.

It's a pretty impressive list so far, isn't it? When I sit and think about all of it, I tend to start feeling a little overwhelmed in a very good way. But there's more, try the rest of these on for size. True intimacy also…

- Plans for our best (Jer 29:11)
- Answers before we call (Isa 65:24)
- Knows my thoughts (Isa 65:24)
- Hears before we speak (Isa 65:24)
- Everlasting love (Jer 31:3)
- Draws us with love/romances us (Jer 31:3)
- Answers us (Jer 33:3)
- Shows us things (Jer 33:3)
- Remain in Him (Jn 15:4-6)
- We are fully present (Jn 15:4-6)
- He searches us (Ps 139)

---

9. Isaiah 26:9

- Knows our anxiety (Ps 139)
- Leads us (Ps 139)
- Knows truth (Jn 8:32)
- Teaches us wisdom (Ps 51:60)
- Repentance (Ps 51)
- Fights for us (Zep 3:17)
- Shouts over (Zep 3:17)
- Quiets us (Zep 3:17)
- Doesn't throw our pasts in our face (Zep 3:17)
- Forgives us (1 Jn 1:9)
- Hairs on our head are numbered (Lk 12:7)
- Died for us (Jn 3:16)
- Listening (Isa 55:3, Pro 2:1-11)
- Created us (Ps 139)
- Never forgets us (Isa 19:15)
- We're beautiful to Him (Song of Solomon)
- Guards our path (Pro 2:1-11)
- Preserves our way (Pro 2:1-11)
- Being still (Ps 46:10)
- Guides (Ps 23:1-6)
- Shields (Ps 23:1-6)
- Gives us rest (Ps 23:1-6)
- Wrestling (Gen 32:22-32)
- Expressing anger (Job, Ps 13)
- Negotiating (Gen 18:16-33)
- Instructs us (2 Tim 3:16)
- Corrects (2 Tim 3:16)
- Trains (2 Tim 3:16)
- Includes my spirit and my brain, my feelings and my intellect. (Matt 22:37)

Looking at this list, what are the facets of intimacy you haven't experienced or have avoided? Which ones have you experienced? Which ones are most appealing to you?

Results of Intimacy

And now, what happens when we begin to experience intimacy with God? What are the results and the things you can expect to see in your life and finances? Let's look at another list. This list of items is really powerful because whatever you need from it can be personally tailored to you and what you need in your life.

Results/Fruit of Intimacy:

- Confidence (Heb 10:19-20)
- Full freedom (Heb 10: 19-20)
- Abundant life (Jn 10:10)
- Experience His resurrection power (Phil 3:10)
- His words are precious (Ps 139:17)
- Praise (Ps 139:17)
- Guarantee of glory (Col 1:24-27)
- Quiet in His love, no anxiety (Zep 3:17)
- Restores us (Rev 3:20)
- Eternal (abundant) life (Jn 10:27-28)
- Deprives evil of power (Col 3)
Understanding, wisdom, and discernment (Pro 2:1-11)
- Absolute trust (Ps 9:10). When I have been through experiences with someone, I come to know their heart fully. I trust

them because I've seen them react. I know their motives and what they're going to do in a given situation. The other day, I was upset and crawled into bed with my husband. I didn't say anything, but after a moment, he simply said, "I'm listening." My husband and I snuggle just about every day, and we don't always talk, but because he knows me, he knew something was wrong. There is a deep level of trust between us. A result of intimacy with God is the same, and there is such a deep level of peace in it!

- Speak with confidence and courage (2 Cor 3:12). How many of you have felt like you've lost your voice? Or maybe you grew up in a church where women weren't supposed to have a voice at all? Intimacy with God gives us our voice! It clarifies who and what we are and gives us the boldness to speak that out over others. To bring clarity and wisdom to difficult situations and to do it with an ease that comes from knowing you are speaking with all the power and backing of the creator of the universe!

- Liberty (2 Cor 3:12)
- Continue to transform into glory (2 Cor 3:18)
- We see the truth of our faults and have access to the power to change (Isa 6:5)
- Endless flow of the Holy Spirit (Jn 4:13-14)
- We have authority to know His will and ask for whatever we want or need within it (Jn 15:7)
- Integrity and courage (2 Tim 3:16)
- We have everything we need for a dynamic and powerful

spiritual life (2 Pet 1:3)
- Goodness, mercy, and love follow us (Ps 23)
- Protection from fear (Ps 23)
- We are led (Ps 23)
- Our life is restored (Ps 23)

Authority looks like this list! Talk about power! Take a moment to picture what your finances and life looks like when you move into this reality! The great news is, as a believer, this is God's plan for you. Wherever you're going, as you abide in Christ and delve deeper into intimacy, these are guaranteed to be the results you'll begin to see in your life, and they will never stop increasing.

Now for those of you who have experienced abuse, it's important to note that you may have a visceral fear response to the idea of intimacy because "intimacy" has harmed you. It can feel terrifying to think of engaging in it. Human intimacy is a different bear…trust the process and know that intimacy with God protects you from 'harmful' intimacy. Once you've experienced the real thing, you will find it easier to discern when someone has harmful motives and give yourself space to process after having intimate time with God or other humans. It will feel good but may also feel exhausting. Rest is good.

We've talked about things that increase intimacy, but we also want to look at some things that kill intimacy. We need to talk about a very simple, powerful tool to address these obstacles. We'll talk about 4 categories of habits that get in the way of intimacy. The first is religious busyness. This one is especially sneaky because it masquerades as a good thing.

Roadblocks to Intimacy

When we're in religion, there is generally an unending list of behaviors we have to engage in in order to be "good enough." Leif Hetland says, "In religion we work FOR love instead of working FROM love." There tends to be an arrogance over the ability to juggle all these rules. This arrogance covers deep shame and fear of what will happen if a ball gets dropped. Now please, don't misunderstand me here and think I'm saying religion is bad. Religion, just like money, is a tool. It is meant to be a vehicle in which we connect with God and each other. The religion I'm talking about here is something that just takes the form of unending tasks and makes someone feel they are in right standing as long as they show up for service and try to be a good person. Any religion operating outside of intimate connection and a relationship with God is just another idol. And the fruit is going to be just as bad, or worse, than someone smoking crack on the corner. I realize that statement might be controversial, but I have yet to find the addict who doesn't realize, deep down, that there is something deeply broken in their lives. They may not admit it readily, but they generally realize they won't be able to break the cycle they're in without help. Religion isn't like that. Religion makes people think that they don't need a relationship. I believe the reason God seems to hate pride so much is because it is the one thing that most consistently keeps people out of intimacy with Him. And religion is full of pride. In Scripture, the people who lived like this were the only people Jesus ever attacked. This seems to demonstrate that this prideful characteristic in religion is more problematic than stealing or prostitution! As we move into talking about other areas getting in the way of intimacy, you'll notice they are obvious things to us. We know we shouldn't do them. But busyness and religion masquerade as good things.

Another issue causing problems for growing in intimacy is doubt. Picture a new relationship with your dream guy. They are everything you hoped for, but because of trauma in your past, you find yourself thinking they're too good to be true. When they take you out to your favorite restaurant, you question their motives. You constantly question what they say, looking for discrepancies, and you find yourself cyber-stalking them to find out what they're "really doing." Do you see this as a relationship with growing intimacy, or will it eventually fall apart? The same is true with our relationship with God. It's easy for our humanity to doubt because Scripture paints a picture of a world that is hard to believe in humanity's beauty and love. Just like the new love who is everything you ever dreamed of, that's who God is to us. Part of the journey is growing in trust as you experience the goodness of God.

Sometimes Christians teach that, because we walk by faith, we're supposed to blindly accept things that don't make sense. This is ridiculous! If my husband said something that doesn't make sense to me, I ask him about it because he is an intimate part of my life and I want to understand what he means! The same is true of God. There is a difference here, though. Pastor Bill Johnson said in a sermon that we are crazy if we don't have questions. Questions aren't the problem. He said questions coming from a place of doubt lead to depression, and questions that come from a place of trust lead to revelation. Questions and doubt are different. Bring your questions to God with confidence, knowing there is an answer. If you feel doubt or skepticism, ask Him for help with that.

Unforgiveness can hinder us from getting rid of fear. This can hinder intimacy as well. I encourage you to take it a step further by making a comprehensive list of resentments and grudges and walking through the same process.

The last issue we'll talk about briefly as an intimacy block with God is compulsive behavior or addictions. Most people view addictions or compulsive behavior as the main problem. They cause quite a bit of chaos, so it's an easy mistake to make! But just like we talked about at the beginning of the book, in order to change our financial story, we need to look at the root of our financial "tree." The same is true of addictions. The root issue of any addiction is an intimacy disorder. We connect with a substance or behavior, so we don't have to face the fear of real intimacy. Because somewhere in our history lies an experience that poisoned our root system and made us believe real intimacy (into me see) isn't safe. When I was in private practice, I had to regularly remind my clients who were in recovery from addictions that healthy intimacy, even when it felt good, would initially be exhausting until they became used to what healthy intimacy looked like.

Intimacy is what we ache for and weren't designed to live without. Because we want and need it so badly, diving into intimacy when we've not understood (or had healthy models) of what it looks like can be terrifying. Make sure to allow yourself time to process and rest as you focus on intimacy.

One Simple Solution

You shall know the truth and the truth will set you free (John 8:32). Showing up and telling the truth is the antidote for any issue around intimacy. Let me say that again because it is the only thing you need to know to be set free. Showing up and telling the truth is the antidote for any issue around intimacy. Intimacy with God and intimacy with others. Give yourself permission to act out if you must, but before acting out in any addiction or self-defeating behavior, show up and tell the truth about what is going on in your heart and head. You'll be shocked to see what a difference it makes.

The 12-step movement is one of the most famous and arguably effective programs for ending addiction behavior. It is quoted in the readings at the beginning of almost every meeting that the only people they've seen be unable to get sober are those who are "constitutionally incapable of being honest." I had a client many years ago who struggled with heroin addiction. Addiction feeds on hiding and dishonesty, so that was a core problem for her as well. Her stories never lined up, and when gently confronted, she would come up with another story that didn't line up. We kept in touch over the years, and she was consistently in and out of treatment. A few years ago, she passed away. You might not be shooting heroin, but whatever your struggle with intimacy is, your door to freedom lies in simply showing up and telling the truth to God, to yourself, and to the safe people around you.

Change Your $tory

Chapter 6
Investment/Education

You were gifted for something. Find it and do it.

The initial chapters of this book are the really important factors. They are the strong foundation you need to change your financial story from the root system so you can find lasting change and authority in your finances. Once you get to that place, I've found many of my clients have questions about what to do next. One client said to me a few months after the live workshop, "I'm not afraid about money anymore, but I'm still not really sure what to do with it." The chapter that follows is NOT a guide about specific investments to make. That is something you'll need to do with someone who is trained, understands Kingdom concepts, and will encourage you to practice your listening skills! If you'd like, you can go to my website (www.changeyourfinancialstory.com/resources) to find some resources I personally trust. But what this chapter will do is possibly reframe some ideas you've had about investing and education when it comes to finances.

In high school, I worked for one of my teachers for a while. He was my coach and PE teacher, and he had a small clock shop where he took in repairs and sold clocks. Even though he and his wife were both teachers, they seemed to be a lot more comfortable financially than our family was. Their three children were all friends of mine, and in the summers, they had their own landscaping business. When their son, Justin, bought a new Mustang in his sophomore year, rumor had it he paid cash. It was the first time I remember thinking that, despite similar circumstances, something was working differently for them. Later on, I realized the difference was in how they invested their time and money. Prior to that, investing wasn't even on my radar. I tended to think of it as being something for greedy people and involved picking the right stocks.

What does Scripture say about this topic? Our beliefs about this area will shape our decisions and future. As was mentioned earlier, there are not many references in Scripture about investing, so we will focus on one in particular that has a great depth of insight in this area.

> It's also like a man going off on an extended trip. He called his servants together and delegated responsibilities. To one he gave five thousand dollars, to another two thousand, to a third one thousand, depending on their abilities. Then he left. Right off, the first servant went to work and doubled his master's investment. The second did the same. But the man with the single thousand dug a hole and carefully buried his master's

Investment/Education

money. After a long absence, the master of those three servants came back and settled up with them. The one given five thousand dollars showed him how he had doubled his investment. His master commended him: "Good work! You did your job well. From now on be my partner." The servant with the two thousand showed how he also had doubled his master's investment. His master commended him: "Good work! You did your job well. From now on be my partner." The servant given one thousand said, "Master, I know you have high standards and hate careless ways, that you demand the best and make no allowances for error. I was afraid I might disappoint you, so I found a good hiding place and secured your money. Here it is, safe and sound down to the last cent." The master was furious. "That's a terrible way to live! It's criminal to live cautiously like that. If you knew I was after the best, why did you do less than the least? The least you could have done would have been to invest the sum with the bankers, where at least I would have gotten a little interest. Take the thousand and give it to the one who risked the most. And get rid of this "play-it-safe" who won't go out on a limb. Throw him out into utter darkness.[1]

The IVP Bible Background Commentary tells us a few important details about this story. At that time, 5,000 talents (dollars in the translation above) was estimated to be

---

1. Matthew 25:14-30, MSG

about 50,000 denarii. One denarius was a day's wage. Even the servant entrusted with a "little" was given almost three years' worth of wages to manage. It would have to be a very wealthy landowner to refer to it as "little." But then again, who is wealthier than God?! The other thing to think about is that, with those amounts of money, the landowner would only give it to very trusted servants to manage. If we take this analogy into our relationship with God, it means the "servants" are those of us who profess to follow and serve God. This is very direct feedback about how we handle money. All the resources are His, He generously gives them to us to manage, according to our ability, and we are to steward them. Before you begin to think, "Well, I must not have the ability for it, so I'm going to have to stay stuck where I am." Is that a belief that lines up with who God says you are? If you aren't sure, let me just tell you, it's not! You are fearfully and wonderfully made, and you can do ALL THINGS through Christ who strengthens you. Even if you are less skilled in managing money than some, remember, the master gave a large amount of resources to the less skilled servant. And the really good news is that skills can be taught! Once you begin to invest and partner with God, He will give you more, and you will grow in your skillset.

Maybe there are others of you like me. When I first began to study the parable, I had the rather sarcastic thought that it would have been handy if the Bible mentioned how exactly the servants could get a 50 percent return on their money. As it turns out, the *IVP Bible Background Commen-*

tary tells us. The servants likely loaned the money with a supremely high-interest rate. Most individuals in that time were not wealthy enough to lend money, so those who did were able to command a great return. The other likely option was that they lent it to money changers, a currency exchange of sorts. The same commentary points out that the servants did not have to work too hard to get this level of return, making the last servant's timidity particularly bad. He would have had to purposely not try because burying money was the "safest" but least effective way to manage money. He basically said to his master, "I don't care." When you are listening to God's direction on how to steward finances, it isn't hard. It is a simple process of seeking God and doing what He guides you to do. This gives an incredible edge over individuals who aren't seeking God and are trying to figure out which investments to make.

The servant also cites fear as his motivation for burying the money. It is interesting to note that the master had no patience for this issue. What is so fascinating about this passage is the master seems to have preferred the servant take a risk, step out in faith and lose the money, rather than cower in fear and do nothing. This aspect of the story should be a great comfort to those who are new to this way of thinking and nervous about losing money in new ventures.

Keith Cunningham, a very wealthy man in his own right (who lost 100 million dollars in business and then made it back), shared the personal tactic he uses when deciding about investments. He says to ask the following questions: What is the upside? What is the downside? Can I live with the downside? I love the simplicity of these questions!

Another way of looking at these questions can be found in Scripture. "Is there anyone here who, planning to build a new house, doesn't first sit down and figure the cost so you'll know if you can complete it? If you only get the foundation laid and then run out of money, you're going to look pretty foolish. Everyone passing by will poke fun at you: 'He started something he couldn't finish.' Or can you imagine a king going into battle against another king without first deciding whether it is possible with his ten thousand troops to face the twenty thousand troops of the other? And if he decides he can't, won't he send an emissary and work out a truce[2]?".

Count the cost when you are thinking about investments. None are guaranteed (this is actually a good way to determine if something is a con or not. If someone says it's a guarantee, it's probably best to run the other way!). It is important to know if you can live with the outcome should the investment not work out. This concept also needs to be combined with the idea of obedience. We started this journey with a focus on listening to God. Marcel and I have had times where we felt God was asking us to invest in something that wasn't anything we would have chosen based on logic. What do you do with the two different messages? One mes-

---

2. Luke 14:28-32, MSG

sage states you should use logic and think things through to make a decision. The other one is based solely on listening to God and doing what you feel led to do, whether it makes sense logically or not.

God encourages us to use our brains. He made them. But it is important to remember that what He says always trumps our logic. His thoughts are not our thoughts. In your walk with Him, you will find He will often direct you to do things that do not make sense to you, logically. Do it anyway. You will also find, as you mature in your faith, there will be times when you ask for direction, and He will encourage you to do what *you'd* like to do. When you're walking closely with Him, your desires will be like His. Thus, you can move forward with confidence. All of this depends on hearing His voice, so if you don't feel this has happened for you yet, I encourage you to revisit the chapter on listening and do the exercises in it. Everything rests on the foundation of listening to God's voice.

Picking Investments

Conventional wisdom tells us the way to work with investments is to figure out what will bring the best return on your money. This is an obvious thought process, given the entire reason for investing is to bring a return. I want to flesh this idea out further by looking at the topic from another angle. Many of you have grown up hearing the text, "Train up a child in the way he should go, and when he is old, he will not depart from it[3]". For many of us, this text was used as the reason we were told to get good safe jobs to help us provide for ourselves and our families. This is not a bad idea, but the core of it can have disastrous results. Some of you reading this are in jobs you hate because you were encouraged to get a good safe job rather than doing what God gifted you to do. This text has been misunderstood and misapplied. Strong's Concordance shows us the original language of "the way he should go" means "according to his individual gifts or bent." God placed specific gifts within you when He formed you, and those are meant to inform the choices you make about the direction you should go. This includes the investments you choose. We've talked about the idea of being a steward of God's resources. I am not likely to be a good steward of things I don't care much about. Here's a practical example. A few months into our financial wilderness season, it became clear we would not be able to afford our house payment and were at risk of going into foreclosure if we didn't take action quickly. With my parents' blessing and invitation, we decided to move into their home until we could get back on our feet. I had always been interested in investing in real estate, and we thought that renting out our home would be a good trial run and offer a little extra income.

What we realized was being a landlord is a great deal of work! There are often repairs, questions, and people moving in and out. All of these changes take a good bit of time. After a year or two, we realized we hated being landlords! We

---

3. Proverbs 22:6, NASB

weren't interested in using our time to repair toilets or call contractors who were too busy to stop by and needed a little extra encouragement (i.e, harassment!). We were not good stewards of that investment because we weren't interested in it. It was soon after this realization that we decided to sell the house. And here is where this comes into play concerning the investments you choose. Choose investments according to what you believe in and are passionate about. God's plan for you financially is to steward His resources and live abundantly within your gifts and passion as He directs. When your investments begin to line up with your personal gifts, you will see money flow more easily. And you will find a joy in investing that you may not have expected.

I'd like to highlight the idea of investing as God directs for a moment as well. When we begin to invest in what God has called us to do, we are guaranteed a good return. That may mean investing in yourself, going to school to learn a new skill, hiring a coach or employee, etc. My mentor Pedro Adao talks a lot about believing that God can make us good soil for a harvest and that it's OK and even necessary to invest in ourselves!

Another aspect of this same concept came up recently as our small group spent time with a missionary family from Indonesia. The humility and spiritual depth of the family deeply impacted me. The father shared a story I won't ever forget. He talked about being in an evangelical college. The majority of his professors talked about this issue from the angle of, "Find what you're good at and do it to the glory of God." Sounds great, right? It's similar to what I've been saying! But my new missionary friend said he had another professor who came at it from a different angle. This professor pointed out the gospel commission to "Go into all the world and preach the gospel to all creation[4]". This professor asked them if they felt they were exempt from this. He then pointed out that there are still 4,300 languages with no translations of Scripture! My mind was blown, and I felt very convicted.

It's important here not to get triggered into a religious mindset. I know that some of you have read this story and immediately felt guilty about the vision you've had on your heart that doesn't include translating Scripture in Indonesia. Am I right?! What I want you to remember here is the bottom-line concept of investing in what is important to God. I've written this book with women entrepreneurs and visionaries in mind, and as you build your businesses, I want you to remember to invest in God's priorities, partnering with Him. I know quite a few missionaries who have the heart to go but don't have the financial resources. Go ahead and build your business, girls! Don't feel ashamed to make buckets of money to invest in the kingdom of God!

The Role of Education in Investing in Your Future

I was blessed to be raised by an educator, and I was almost finished with high school before I realized that not

---

4. Mark 16:15, NASB

Investment/Education

everyone gets to go to college. It was not optional in our home. After college, I applied and was accepted to graduate school at Vanderbilt University. I had gone to private Christian schools my entire life and wanted to see if I could cut it in the "Ivy Leagues." I finished this run of educational experience in a great deal of debt, despite being granted a teaching assistantship that could have paid my tuition and living expenses if I had learned the lessons I'm teaching in this book. My beliefs around money had not been healed yet, so I saw the loans as "free money." The financial hole I was in got deeper. I was well-educated and poorer than ever.

It was a funny thing working through all this because as an adult, I realized that if I had enough discipline, I could have learned everything I paid ridiculous sums of money for from my local library. Yes, granted, I could not have gotten the interaction with friends, brilliant professors, and structure. I would not have gotten licensed in my field as a therapist, for those reasons and more, I do not regret my expensive education. But a point I want to make is you do not have to have a degree to become educated. Not all learning (actually very little of it when you add up all the things we learn throughout our lives) comes with an expensive degree. You will always need to invest in education, but that investment can look like an investment of time, an investment of tracking down people who are successful in what you want to do and asking if you can take them to coffee and pick their brain. It may include finding an amazing course advertised on Facebook about a topic you're fascinated with.

The thrilling thing about this type of education is you are the author. You pick the topic, and it is up to you what to study. This means you can tailor the things you learn according to what the Holy Spirit places on your heart and in accordance with the things you're passionate about.

Scriptural Perspectives on Education

It is clear. Scripture is in favor of education. Proverbs 9:9 says, "instruct the wise and they will be wiser still; teach the righteous and they will add to their learning." Proverbs 1:5 says, "Let the wise listen and add to their learning, and let the discerning get guidance." This text infers that knowledge is different from wisdom and discernment. If you struggle with the idea of "being good enough or smart enough" to get the education you need about finances, you can start by asking for wisdom and discernment from God. Scripture tells us that these things lead into knowledge and guidance.

If you tend to feel intimidated about learning, Luke 10:21 (MSG) is a comfort as well. "At that, Jesus rejoiced, exuberant in the Holy Spirit. 'I thank you, Father, Master of heaven and earth, that you hid these things from the know-it-alls and showed them to these innocent newcomers. Yes, Father, it pleased you to do it this way." The things God wants to teach you are things He can reveal even to little children. There is no need for you to feel ashamed or intimidated, no matter what your background is. In fact, you may be more at risk of stumbling in this area if you have a high opinion of your intellect!

Investment/Education

What Should I Learn?

There are millions of books on finances and wealth, and this book's aim is not to teach you everything there is to know about business and money management. This book aims to get you ready to be a good steward of the resources God gives you and be in an emotional place to enjoy it on the way. With that in mind, here are some concepts you will want to consider that will also help you narrow and define what else you need to learn.

1) Identify your "why." What's the motivation for educating yourself? What does your heart beat for in this area? What makes you thrilled? What makes you angry? These will be the things you are most passionate about and areas that will have the ability to capture your attention for a lifetime. It needs to be about your purpose and what God has called you to do. The *why* needs to be bigger than you are, so when things get hard, you will be motivated by things that go beyond you.

2) Identify what you're passionate about. Stewardship and investments demand attention. You will need to pay attention to what is going on with them, and while you may not run the business or investment, it will always be vital for you to understand how they work. If you aren't interested in them, you will likely either resent the time you have to give it, or you will end up not paying attention to it and thus possibly losing money. Investing in projects or companies

that interest you will make this a non-issue. It will also make investment opportunities easier to sift through. If you are new to the idea of investing, start with thinking of the things you enjoy or are knowledgeable about. You will likely draw options from things connected to this list in some way. For example, when I first became investment-minded, I compiled a list of things I enjoyed or had expertise in. This list spanned the large things I spent years training for, to other things I just happened to like (food!). As I brainstormed this list, I thought about all the times at work when I had only ten minutes between clients and was hungry. I asked the director at our private practice how much money they got for every Coke sold from the machine. Then I asked if they would be interested in a machine offering snacks as well, which could pay the practice more than Coca-Cola did. They liked this idea, and our first investment was born. It was a steady source of income for several years. This came simply from identifying my interests as well as the need that I could meet. Don't be fooled by thinking you have to have an MBA to be an investor. There are investments of every size and in every area of interest. And, as Scripture promises, when you are faithful in stewarding what God gives you, He gives you more!

3) The things you've thought on that you are passionate about, prayerfully pick one or more (depending on the time available to you) and start learning everything you can about it. If you are working with things you're interested in, this will not be difficult at all.

4) Don't lose focus. One thing you will realize as you start to become investment-minded is there are literally millions of options out there. It will be important not to run after every opportunity that comes your way. This is where listening to God becomes especially important. You will need to learn to get quiet and listen for His direction with every option that comes your way. Early on in this phase, I was working on a book, building a blog following, holding down a full-time private practice, and had invested in a start-up company with a friend. I was continuously frustrated because I didn't have enough time to do any of it very well and had to make some hard decisions to let some of it go. I was truly interested in all of it, but focus gives us the direction and momentum we need. A lack of focus will ensure you're never fully successful in any area.

5) Know where you're going. In his book *Mentored by a Millionaire*, Steven Scott talks about a process he calls vision mapping. He uses the following story to illustrate the importance of having a clear plan on direction. He poses the following question: If I gave you free tickets to Hawaii to stay at a 15,000 square foot mansion on the beach, I offered you $1000 a day while you were there, and told you that on the counter at the estate is a check in your name for $1,000,000 would you like that? What if I didn't tell you where that estate was though, and you had to find it on your own within 24 hours, or else you would lose the dream vacation and would have to reimburse me for expenses? Would you take that deal? Of course not! It would be impossible to find this dream estate on one of seven islands without a map, plan,

or directions. Scott points out that our lives are no different, but very few people have a plan on how they will reach their goals. What impact do you want to have on the world? Make a plan with the Holy Spirit and strategize with Him to make it happen.

Education will never end. It is part of how God finishes the work He started in us. Begin to think of education as a fun journey of learning about things that God made you good at and passionate about.

Fear of Failure or Success

We spent a good portion of time early on in the book talking about the importance of beliefs. In addressing education, it is important to take note of how you feel about failure or success. As I was finishing this book and beginning work on sharing the workshops, I realized I had a core belief that, if I truly served humanity, it would kill me. This sounds silly and illogical, but when you look at my history, the fear made sense. I grew up in a workaholic family system and culture, and my senior year in high school, I ended up in the hospital with multiple illnesses that were the result of chronic stress. Many years of my healing were devoted to learning balance and self-care. Naturally, when I started to think about God-sized dreams, it brought to mind these issues from my past. I realized I was afraid the call of God would kill me. He was the one who gave me clarity on what I was afraid of. It was not something I had been consciously aware of. If that belief stayed outside my awareness and wasn't dealt with, do you

Investment/Education

think I would successfully move fully into my calling? No! I wouldn't do something that I thought would kill me! The same is true for you. If you have a fear of failure or success that keeps you from the things your heart quietly longs for, the answer to this is to ask God to reveal the beliefs and agreements that keep you from moving toward it. Your life and the lives of the people who need to be touched by your gifts are at stake!

Change Your $tory

Chapter 7
Gratitude/Praise/Play

Praise scatters your enemies while you dance.

Praise has not always come easily for me. I struggled with the idea of a God who demands praise as if He's some sort of narcissist. I have a personality tendency that leans toward introspection. What this means is that the lessons of this chapter have been challenging and hard-fought. Indeed, I am still learning. Whenever I think about praise, I have a strong tendency to avoid the topic if things are not going well. I grew up putting on a good mask much of the time, and it almost killed me. Being authentic and real was a part of what saved me, so I fight against the feeling of being fake with a great passion. My hope is that this chapter will offer confirmation of the vital importance of praise and gratitude and an authentic way to engage in it.

I have a friend named Kathy. Kathy and I have been in a prayer group for years, and we spend a good bit of time together. The first thing that becomes apparent about Kathy when you meet her is how positive and affirming she is. She consistently and honestly looks on the bright side of things, and if you are feeling down or discouraged, she never fails to offer an affirmation that can turn the whole day around. She is naturally a "praiser." After being around her for several years, now I have noticed something else. Whenever there is a drawing for a prize of any kind, it seems Kathy's name is called. I have seen her win hundreds of dollars-worth of prizes over the years. Now I certainly don't have any scientific proof that Kathy wins because of her positive thinking. But I do find it interesting because it matches the information we have about how a life of gratitude impacts us.

The Bible tells us that rejoicing is a safeguard for us[1]. We are to constantly bring our prayers and petitions to God and never forget to thank Him. These three simple steps are a safeguard, and they are how we stand firm in adversity. They also do the double duty of keeping us humble when things are going extremely well. The other amazing thing about rejoicing is that it offers us peace in chaotic circumstances.

When I began writing this book and soon after lost almost all of our income within one week, my first impulse was shock and fear. Before this though, I had been studying the Israelites, praying to come into the promised land God had put on my heart years before. I recognized the opportunity amid the shock. I began to pray I would stand firm during this time and walk through it in peace. A friend shared the above verse in Philippians 3:1 that tells us how to

---

1. Philippians 3:1

stand firm, and it is what I practiced. I learned to show up authentically with God. I practiced telling Him when I was scared, what I was thinking, what I needed, and I learned to end in gratitude and praise. There were moments I was so angry about the journey I resisted practicing this habit, but when I did, I was always at peace.

Years ago, I was speaking with a client who was struggling with the will to live. He was so hurt and disillusioned he was unsure of his purpose or how to survive. We talked about the need to get more support to heal from his past, and I suggested a spiritual retreat center. He was struggling with the idea of taking time off work and the cost of the program. I asked him the question, "How much is peace worth to you?" This completely changed the tone of the conversation, and his resistance crumbled. I believe that the millions of people who struggle with anxiety and fear would give anything to obtain peace. What would it look like to go through tragedy and still have peace? To go through the loss of finances, economic uncertainty, or concern for your children and never lose your peace? Some of you may be frustrated right now and feel this isn't a realistic possibility. It's not logical to say this. It doesn't make sense. Most of what God offers us doesn't make sense. Listen, the promises in the Bible are either true, or they aren't. Even if you're skeptical, try it. See what happens. There is nothing to lose and everything to gain.

Here is another example of the impossible things that happen when we stay in praise and gratitude. 2 Chronicles 20 shares the story of Jehosophat. He was a king who found out from his intelligence officers that three different groups had gathered a huge army to come against the Israelites. Scripture tells us that Jehosophat was shaken and immediately began to pray. He also ordered a nation-wide fast. This was the first illogical thing that happened. Logic dictates the warriors would need all the strength they could get! The entire country gathered together to pray. The king reminded God of His provision in bringing them to that place and acknowledged God's power. He reminded God that no one could come against Him. Then Jehosophat and the people listened and got a word from God from one of the men in the crowd. He told them God had given them the battle and the directions on where to meet their enemies. (Notice that God didn't turn their enemies away, He asked the Israelites to face them and step out in faith in what He said.). The next thing they did was bow down on their faces to worship God, and then they stood up to praise Him.

The next morning the king put together a choir. No offense to the musicians out there, but it would not be my natural inclination to send out the musicians as the first line of defense in this scenario! The choir went out ahead of the army, praising God for His love that never ends. Scripture tells us when they started shouting and praising, God set ambushes, and the men who were coming against them turned on each other and fought themselves.

I imagine there were initially some shaky voices in that choir. I also imagine some in that choir didn't "feel like" praising God. I think this is where the concept of a "sacrifice of praise" comes into place.

God knows the struggle to praise Him when you are hurting, and I believe He honors that. He certainly honored the Israelites. It took them three days to carry the left-over resources off the battle-field. It is in moments like that that praise is not too difficult!

Hebrews 12:28 talks about us having a kingdom that is firm and stable, one that can't be shaken, so because of that, let us be thankful and worship with reverence and awe. I grew up with a lot of intention to follow the Bible, but I never really saw a lot of active faith around me. I didn't experience the Bible's promises as true, although I could fight like a crazy courtroom brawler about theological points. God only knows how many people I turned off. When I began to experience God as having truly saved me, when I went through crises, and He was all I had to hang onto, I began to learn how stable and firm God was. He was teaching me to be stable and firm, too. Because I was in a relationship with Him and practicing trust rather than a 'to-do list of rules,' I began to know certain things were true because they had become heart knowledge. And that was a fulfilled promise as well. God promises to write His promises on our hearts (Hebrews 8:10), and when they are written on our hearts, we don't question them any longer. It has become a thread of knowing in our lives, and from that place, reverence and praise are not things we "should" do. They are things we can't help but do. They flow freely from the heart.

Romans 1:21 talks about knowing God and not being in gratitude. "For although they knew God, they neither glorified Him as God nor gave thanks to Him, but their thinking became futile and their foolish hearts were darkened." This text seems to infer a cause-and-effect relationship. If you feel that, despite your best intentions, you find your thinking scrambled and your heart a dark place, practice some gratitude.

Jesus was an example of this way of being as well. In John 6:5-11 we read the story of feeding the 5,000.

> When Jesus looked up and saw a great crowd coming toward him, he said to Philip, "Where shall we buy bread for these people to eat?" He asked this only to test him, for he already had in mind what he was going to do. Philip answered him, "It would take more than half a year's wages to buy enough bread for each one to have a bite!" Another of his disciples, Andrew, Simon Peter's brother, spoke up, "Here is a boy with five small barley loaves and two small fish, but how far will they go among so many?" Jesus said, "Have the people sit down." There was plenty of grass in that place, and they sat down (about five thousand men were there). Jesus then took the loaves, gave thanks (emphasis added), and distributed to those who were seated as much as they wanted. He did the same with the fish.

Gratitude/Praise/Play

It hit me one day when reading this passage that Jesus gave thanks and didn't even ask for the loaves and fishes to be multiplied. There was power enough in the thanksgiving to obtain what was needed! Food enough to feed 5,000 men plus women and children when in the earth's economy, it would have cost them more than a half-a-year's wages.

How do we come to terms with this concept of being created to praise the Lord when a part of us may whisper that it's pretty arrogant of God to ask for praise? C.S. Lewis struggled with this concept as well and put it this way in his book, *Reflections on the Psalms*[2]:

> But the most obvious fact about praise - whether of God or anything - strangely escaped me. I thought of it in terms of compliment, approval, or the giving of honor. I had never noticed that all enjoyment spontaneously overflows into praise unless…shyness or the fear of boring others is deliberately brought in to check it. The world rings with praise - lovers praising their mistresses [Romeo praising Juliet and vice versa], readers their favorite poet, walkers praising the countryside, players praising their favorite game - praise of weather, wines, dishes, actors, motors, horses, colleges, countries, historical personages, children, flowers, mountains, rare stamps, rare beetles, even sometimes politicians or scholars…except were intolerably adverse circumstances interfere, praise almost

---

2. *C.S. Lewis, Reflections on the Psalms*

seems to be inner health made audible…I had not noticed either that just as men spontaneously praise whatever they value, so they spontaneously urge us to join them in praising it: "Isn't she lovely? Wasn't it glorious? Don't you think that magnificent?" The Psalmists in telling everyone to praise God are doing what all men do when they speak of what they care about. My whole, more general, difficulty about the praise of God depended on my absurdly denying to us, as regards the supremely valuable, what we delight to do, what indeed we can't help doing, about everything else we value…I think we delight to praise what we enjoy because the praise not merely expresses but completes the enjoyment; it is its appointed consummation.

God asks for praise in the same way. I love it when my husband, who I love very much, praises me. I care about what he thinks of me. God cares what we think of Him. Out of my love for my husband comes a natural tendency - indeed, I can't stop myself - to tell the world how incredible he is. This is the source of our praise as well, and there is immense power in it. I used to think praise meant I had to fake it and parrot words I didn't really feel or believe. Have you ever had someone say something nice to you that you knew they didn't mean? Nobody likes that, and God is no different. When you practice praise, be authentic. Also know that, as you listen to Him, as you see miracles happen and your $tory change, it will get easier and easier!

Gratitude/Praise/Play

Change Your $tory

Conclusion

When you begin to adjust your beliefs to be in line with what God says, listen to God, and when you refuse the lies that Satan offers that lead to shame and fear, your $tory will change completely. There is work in it, and changing our beliefs sometimes means sorting through some pain in our past. But wouldn't you deal with a little pain to get everything your soul longs for? To not have to beat down the voices in your head that shame you? To be free? To have peace, joy, and confidence? To do what thrills you rather than being tied to a job you aren't passionate about? The exciting news is, as you take the steps in this book, things change around your finances almost without notice. Doing the right thing becomes effortless (admittedly, I still hate the detail work of paying bills, and I will likely never balance a checkbook. But the shame is gone around those things, leaving me free to find solutions that work for how God designed me), and there is peace in knowing that if you do get stuck or stumped, there is an unlimited resource of wisdom and provision right at your fingertips.

I hope you have enjoyed this book and that you implement the concepts in it. I don't know your specific situation, but I do know you have hopes and dreams, something you were meant to do, and money is a part of that. Getting a clear picture of what role it plays and how to manage it will change everything. You've probably already noticed that this book could be about other topics as well. The principles are universal whether you are talking about money or relationships. When you practice the principles and make them a part of your heart, you will see improvements in other areas of your life as well. Think of it as a bonus! You were meant for abundance, and when you lean into God, you will begin to see it flow everywhere.

I hope you will continue your Change Your $tory journey. Interact with us on Facebook at the Change Your $tory page or sign up for our email list at www.changeyourfinancialstory.com to be notified of upcoming events. Your stories are the reason we do this, and they fuel our fire as well.

Change Your $tory

Made in the USA
Middletown, DE
05 May 2022